SHOW US
YOUR WITS

Dear Mate,
  enjoy! Just a little
distraction 😊

Happy Birthday (2020)

ALSO BY THE SYNDROME MAG

Random Female Syndromes

SHOW US YOUR WITS

FUNNY WOMEN SURVIVING THE COVID CRISIS BY LAUGHING THROUGH IT

EDITED BY: SILVIA BAJARDI, LEIGH ANNE JASHEWAY, CHIKA EKEMEZIE AND CARMEN WOODRUFF

Published by The Syndrome Mag
Seattle, WA
www.thesyndromemag.com

Interior layout and design by www.writingnights.org
Book preparation by Chad Robertson
Cover design by Ivica Jandrijevic

ISBN: 978-1-7363037-0-2
LIBRARY OF CONGRESS CATALOGING-IN-PUBLICATION DATA:
NAMES: Silvia Bajardi, Leigh Anne Jasheway, Chika Ekemezie
and Carmen Woodruff, editors
TITLE: Show Us Your Wits – Funny Women Surviving Coronavirus by
Laughing through It / The Syndrome Magazine
DESCRIPTION: Show us Your Wits is a collection of essays from women
across the world who are coping with quarantine, social distancing, tele-
working, and all the other COVID-19 changes we're facing. These hys-
terical first-person stories chronicle a year of unprecedented global challenges, and by sharing them, we all become more connected in a multigen-
erational, multicultural community. So mask up and sit tight. Because
how the hell else are we supposed to get through it?
IDENTIFIERS: ISBN 978-1-7363037-0-2 (Perfect bound) |
SUBJECTS: | Feminist Theory | Humor | Covid 19 Pandemic |
Classification: Pending
LC record pending

24   23   22   21   20   8   7   6   5   4   3   2   1

DEDICATION

To our sisters and feminist allies who have survived a global pandemic while schooling their children, clocking in at their jobs, avoiding becoming Stepford Wives, spending countless hours online scrolling through for unwatched Netflix shows, running for office, day drinking, saying a final farewell to high heels, flirting with delivery folks, helping feed the hungry, wondering what shade of eyeshadow looks best with a facemask, Zoom calling until they dream in grids, attending to their pet's every need, and most of all...laughing their way through it all.

CONTENTS

ALSO BY THE SYNDROME MAG...II

DEDICATION..V

CONTENTS..VI

INTRODUCTION...1

APPEARANCE...5

I'm Your Favorite Leggings; Let Me Die with Dignity **by Gracie Kairis** 7

Using My Roots to Measure Time by **Taylor Griggs** 9

My Hijab is My Decision, Not Yours by **Aaesha A.**.....................................12

50 Shades of Athleisure **by Kathryn Sadakierski**......................................15

The Ugly Stages of Quarantine:
From Duck Heads to Stripper Poles **by Kristen Ferreira**...........................18

Fashion & Make-Up Tips for Going Back to the Office **by Ellie Connor** 21

FAMILY AND PARENTING..27

The Quarantine Quickie: How One Mom Coped
with COVID-19 Lockdown in Spain **by Linda Freund** 29

Bougie "Baaji": Lessons in Intersectionality
from the Lockdown **by Sarah Shamim** 33

Finally, The Perfect Time to Have a Baby **by Naomi Fitter**..........................36

Sleeping with the Cat **by Meg Riley**..39

Bee Calm and Carry On **by Daien Guo**..42

The Now Times **by Adina Gillett**..45

A Theatrical Scene Between my 3-Year-Old and Me: By an Unemployed
Playwright **by Laura Wheatman Hill**.. 49

Surviving Quicksand in the Age of Quarantine **by Laura Iodice**.................52

Breastfeeding Tips with Mr. Sloth **by Sara Savusa** 55

Pandemic Syndrome Retirement **by Patricia Florio** 58

Tips from Italy: How to Survive
the COVID-19 Lockdown with a Teenager **by Katherine Wilson** 61

WORK AND SCHOOL **67**

Fact-Checking: The Truth Will Set You Free...
Until it Won't **by Fernanda Estrada Argumedo**............................... 69

Lost in Translation **by Brooke Stanicki**...................................72

Zooming in, Tuning Out **by Anndee Hochman** 75

Welcome to Virtual Hell:
Nursing School in the Age of COVID-19 **by Alexandra Nicole Benson**....79

Pandemic Got Your Job? No Worries:
Quarantine Skills to Beef Up Your Resume **by Eloise O'Loane**................. 83

Selling Pot During COVID-19 **by Jamie Colson**............................... 86

COMMUNITY...**91**

Pandemic Party **by Marie Steinwachs** 93

A Non-Aggressive Video Chat Invitation **by Halle Zander** 97

The Jackals **by Lauren Klein**... 99

A Dog's Life, Or Is it My Life? **by Adina Gillett**...........................103

Rockin' in the Un-Free World **by Bethany Grace Howe**...........................107

The Hill **by Chika Ekemezie** 110

RELATIONSHIPS AND SEX...**113**

How to Keep Your Marriage Alive
(In the Time of COVID) **by Laura Wheatman Hill**.............................115

The Quick and Dirty Guide to Dating Apps:

Global Pandemic Edition **by Hayley Zablotsky** 117

Porn in Lockdown: An Italian Woman's
(Not-so) Guilty Pleasure **by Laura Magnani**.................................. 121

We Don't Get to Pick Our Quarantine (S)heroes **by Joanna Collins** 124

A Digital Dating Doozy and Other Online Disasters **by Carmen Woodruff** . 128

Relationship Advice for Sheltering in Place **by Lori Barrett** 131

MENTAL HEALTH AND WELLNESS **135**

A Coronavirus Yoga Practice **by Wendy BooydeGraaff** 137

I Won't Drink to That **by Melody Dodd** 140

Extrovert Loses Mind Hours into Social Distancing **by Kate R. Canter** ... 142

Five Ways to Stay a Bad-Ass Bitch
in a Coronavirus World **by Christie Withanie**................................144

Four Signs Quarantine Has Gotten To You **by Mia DeSantis** 146

Quarantine Dream Interpretation **by Regina Velázquez** 149

Five Ways to Use Male Ego
Against Your Abuser During Lockdown **by Giugi Carminati** 154

Unhealthy Ways I'm Dealing with this Crisis **by Daphne Dot**....................157

My Weird Quarantine Diary **by Stacey Gustafson** 160

Another Milestone Birthday **by Katie Glauber Bush** 164

SURVIVING QUARANTINE **169**

The TP-ing Point **by Bethany Grace Howe** 171

Substitutions Made by Your Instacart Shopper **by Courtney Watson** 174

Quarantined in the Kitchen **by Ariel Balter** 176

Mother Earth: It's Not Quarantine –
It's Time Out for Bad Children **by Leigh Anne Jasheway** 179

Grocery Store Battle **by Jennifer Scully** 182

Pandemic Lockdown:
It's Better than an Iranian Prison Cell **by Jasmine Eftekhari**......................184

Homelessness, Queer Kids and COVID-19 **by Belinda Carroll**.................187

The London Flu **by Rochelle Asquith**...190

Advice for Surviving Lockdown from
The *Miss Congeniality* Movies **by Leigh Anne Jasheway** 193

Grocery Store Battle – Did I mention
that I am Chinese-American? **by Christina Tang-Bernas** 196

I'm Not Ready to Die **by Linda White** 200

CONTRIBUTORS 203
ACKNOWLEDGEMENTS 211
ABOUT US: THE SYNDROME MAG...213
DONATE..214
CREDITS 215

INTRODUCTION

Do you really have to read an introduction to enjoy the pleasure of reading a book?

Definitely not.

So, go ahead; just skip it. I won't be offended.

Or: start from the cover. Then skip ahead to the contents, and then peruse the biographies at the end. Picture the women who made these stories possible; hear them laugh themselves breathless. You'll chuckle with them on an extraordinary ride that will transport you through time and space.

But first things first. Why this cover?

The women who work on *The Syndrome* team think that making inequalities visible helps to promote gender equality.

And so there you have it, more obvious than a jumbo screen in Times Square. Let your eyes linger freely on the curves, the masks!

We've replaced the classic cat call, a vulgarity dressed up as a compliment—that somehow justifies or condones a culture of violence—with a loud and clear: "Show us your wits." Why pair these elements with COVID-19? Because the past year has exacerbated the gender gap when it comes to employment, health, unpaid labor, and increased violence against women and girls. But the pandemic has also highlighted another thing: female ingenuity. That is exactly what this book is about: the convergence between the emergency and a search for opportunities, between the hard unpredictability of this contagion and personal initiative.

It's what we can keep under control when the world is out of control, starting with a well-made banana bread. We do it while laughing and staying connected through technology or merely behind our masks. Laughing with another person is one of the most universal and often-times surprising ways we have of connecting with one another.

While consumerism and globalization have halted, preventing us from traveling, buying things, and going places, the everyday life field of action is narrowing around the domestic sphere, and women are becoming its crux once again, like it or not. They switch from psychologist to teacher to nurse and back while simultaneously directing children, pets, and work-related video conferences with professional aplomb, despite being in pajamas and strategizing how to come out on top when the next toilet paper raid takes over the neighborhood Costco.

Though the pandemic has leveled the world under a single threat, its impact is different from person to person. Between racial, ethnic, cultural and national groups, our differences and privileges have further polarized us. Women are the ones who pay the highest price.

What emerges from these stories, which bring together a multiplicity of voices and countries, is the will to not let ourselves be overwhelmed by these events, and more than anything, not to let fear define us. Because no matter the circumstance, laughing wildly—no holds barred, bras to the wind—is what keeps us alive.

The Directress

Appearance

I'M YOUR FAVORITE LEGGINGS; LET ME DIE WITH DIGNITY

by Gracie Kairis

Hey, it's me, your favorite pair of black leggings. We need to have a serious talk. We've had some good times. I will never forget the day eight years ago when you brought me home from Old Navy or all of the Tinder dates you wore me on. And now, after all those times I've been there for you, I'm asking you to be there for me: Please put me out of my misery.

My quality of life is dismal at this point. My elastic is stretched beyond repair. My legs are covered with little thread pills and we both know that hole in my crotch is not getting any smaller.

I probably would have had another good two years in me, but you have been pushing me so hard in quarantine. I used to seamlessly transition from a day to night look, but you've taken that to the extreme by wearing me four days in a row, 24 hours a day. You haven't even taken me off to shower or change your underwear. What ponte knit pant could be expected to thrive under these conditions? I have gone downhill rapidly to terminally threadbare.

In my heyday, I flattered your figure, no matter how bloated you were from bingeing on Cheez-Its, but I am now stretched way beyond capacity. I love you, but when you ordered and then ate an entire Walmart sheet cake while crouching on the couch with your knees tucked underneath you like Gollum, you did irreparable damage to my structural integrity. Every frosting-drenched fiber of my poly-cotton blend is screaming out for the sweet release of death.

Please don't try to prolong my life. I know you're thinking that maybe you can summon the strength to peel me off your body, then throw me in the washing machine with a scoop of Oxiclean and a prayer. At best, I could only survive another week of your current lifestyle. And at what cost? I don't want to leave this world a catastrophic, humiliating failure. I'm but one deep squat to check the back of the shelf at Safeway for toilet paper away from ripping into an irreparable chasm, baring your cotton granny panties for all to see. I implore you to let me go now, while one of us still has a shred of dignity.

For my service, I don't want anything too fancy. Maybe sing a few bars of "Wind Beneath My Wings" and show a tasteful slideshow of all the Instagram photos where you're wearing me "on your way to yoga," but you were actually going to Chipotle. (Don't worry, I will be taking that to my grave.) I know social distancing makes it impossible for people to attend my funeral, I hope my two closest companions, your Bearpaw house slippers and your boyfriend's over-sized Miami Dolphins sweatshirt, will attend. They've been there nearly every day during these last difficult weeks, suffering right alongside me.

When I'm gone, I want you to find new leggings. (Preferably soon, as I honestly don't know what you'll cover yourself with when I'm no longer around.) You may think that you'll never find a pair as reliable as me, but before you know it, you'll have new go-to bottoms to break-in and eventually ruin with your slovenly behavior.

I don't know if there's an afterlife for leggings, but if there is, I like to think that I will be re-made of a more breathable, moisture-wicking celestial fabric and that there are no cats around to constantly poke me full of tiny holes. It's time for me to say goodbye, and for you to shepherd me into the next life, as difficult as this task may be. I am at peace and ready for a dignified eternal rest in that great big dresser drawer in the sky.

Wait, is that a Goodwill Donation Center?

You monster.

USING MY ROOTS TO MEASURE TIME

by Taylor Griggs

It's late November. I've begun to measure time by pressing my hair down against my scalp and leaning my forehead against the mirror, fogging it with my breath as I estimate how long my roots are. The last time I bleached my hair was in July, I think—yes, I remember the burning that made my ears tear up, the fumes starting to disintegrate my frontal lobe as I watched my dark roots start to lighten. This looks like, what, two and a half inches? That seems right.

When I first bleached my hair this year, it felt inevitable. Destroying your hair during a global pandemic is the natural progression of the path for all 23-year-olds who know why Manic Pixie Dream Girls are harmful but still sort of want to be one. I had almost grown out all the bleach from the last time I fucked up my hair, and had sworn to leave it alone until it was healthy again, but I found myself on the phone with the Sally Beauty employee making a bleach order for curbside pickup.

It was April, right in the midst of the spring quarantine, and I was unemployed and living at my parents' house, trying to go viral on Tik-Tok like it was my job. My mom, remembering how I'd openly expressed so much regret after last bleaching my hair—"My curls! My dry ends!"—shook her head and put up her hands. My dad asked me to please put down a towel so I wouldn't ruin the bathroom tile.

That first trip to Sally's didn't get the job done, so I became a regular, along with the other people who'd deluded themselves into thinking that coloring your hair is "essential" during a global pandemic. I'd sit in the bathroom for hours at a time, mixing powders and gels like a 16th century alchemist, watching hour-long YouTube videos about celebrity drama that I didn't care about.

Even after bleaching it so many times, combining the powder and smearing it across my hairline, trying to distract myself from the stinging pain, it still always felt like magic to watch the hair turn white. In a world that was crumbling at the seams, I found a sense of purpose in working toward the concrete goal of getting my hair to be a certain color. I felt like an artist, albeit one with obvious addictions to shopping and getting likes on Instagram.

I kept this up for a couple months after I left my parents' house, but without their mild pestering, I lost interest. I became obsessed with the thrilling contrast between the dark roots and bleached ends, noticing that I could tangibly see how long my hair was getting by monitoring how ugly it was.

I've spent so much of my life desperately yearning for time to work the way I want it to, begging, fruitlessly, for solutions to the painful nostalgia that asks me to look backwards all the time, eschewing "zen" in favor of constant worrying.

And as everyone is constantly reminding each other, repeating the same joke about how we'll always be stuck in March 2020, time is even weirder this year. Without the typical annual landmarks—the first backyard party to celebrate the summer, going to crowded movie theaters on July afternoons to beat the heat, freezing on the walk to a Halloween party, being annoyed with your family on Thanksgiving—life is just a blur.

I haven't been keeping up a regular journal, and I frequently forget to change the page on my decorative calendar that I bought in the naive month of January 2020. But even if I can remind myself that an entire, pandemic-filled year has almost passed, it's hard to conceptualize what that really means.

Being able to see my hair grow, knowing that it keeps getting longer even as I sit inside for weeks on end, doing nothing but worrying and not drinking enough water, is comforting. I don't know what a day or a week or a month feels like, but I know what growing a half-inch of hair looks like.

I like having visible proof that my body has been doing something productive even when my brain feels like mush. You can't see your cells reproducing, your blood flowing through your veins, your kidney do-ing...whatever it does. You can see your hair growing, especially if you're looking for it.

Maybe I just brought my hair to the brink of death in order to chase the high of nursing it back to health. And I got a few Instagram likes out of it too. So what? It's not the worst thing you could be doing during a global pandemic.

MY HIJAB IS MY DECISION, NOT YOURS

by Aaesha A.

The entire world has been preoccupied masking up to protect themselves from an invisible bug spreading faster than particles from an openmouthed sneeze…on a windy day. As a non-white American-born Muslim woman of Indian descent who consciously puts considerable thought into her daily attire in attempts to not look, as Trump or his minions would call, "too Muslim," just the thought of having to add a face mask on top of it all has been absolutely dreadful.

A simple run to the store no longer exists and in fact has turned into my worst nightmare, right alongside needing to schedule an appointment for my wisdom teeth removal, two decades too late. Showing up in a fashionable outfit on a body that is attached to a hijab-laden head is often a problem for onlookers. Forgotten are manners while staring or making rude comments, all of which I pretend to not see or hear, yet all are felt. I am human after all, in case they missed that while being consumed by the soft-colored fabric on my head.

To be completely honest, I live two separate lives, each with its own purpose. One is reserved for my morning jogs when all I want to do is hide and clear my head from life and all its crazies. Slapping on a cap, hoodie, shades, and headphones, you don't see me; I don't see you. The other is where I dress knowing full well that I will be watched and judged. I embrace my American-Muslim identity, choosing to equally represent both the American and the Muslim within. Ideally, I would want nothing more than to steer clear of attracting attention (severely introverted here) but since the hijab on my head is nothing short of a giant neon sign with bright flashing lights screaming "LOOK AT ME!" and because being a visible Muslim makes all of my personal actions and words somehow directly linked to represent the nearly two billion Muslims in the world, my guard must always be up, and I most certainly am never allowed a bad day. Ever.

Recently, I learned something new about the world, entirely by chance. It was on a day when I had come home from my morning run, and my children, desperate for a proper breakfast of milk and eggs, begged me to go and pick some up. Unlike the many versions of exotic breads I had managed to whip up during my time in quarantine, neither milk nor eggs would yield successful results despite my endless attempts. Having had no luck with Amazon Prime's promise for a two-hour delivery window, then unavailable for the foreseeable future, I would have no choice but to mask up and stand in line to acquire those curious, judgmental, trying-to-be-discrete-but-failing-at glances which I had not missed at all during my two-month long retreat in my cave. With a deep sigh, (and a reminder to my children that they owed me for life), I turned and left. Milk and eggs. Just milk and eggs.

I waited a half an hour in line before my spot was up front. The man at the door was extra chipper today, more than I had ever experienced, perhaps the warm California sunshine was doing it for him. He ushered me in with a "Hello, welcome!" and "Enjoy your day, Miss!" This was new.

There were markings on the floor letting shoppers know which aisles were for entering and which were not. I only needed to get to the back of the store, milk and eggs were my goal. Certain that nobody would care this time if I went the wrong way, I did just that. A man bending down to grab a bag of marshmallows looked up and asked me if he was in MY way. "Just let me know and I'll move my cart." Umm, OK. Thanks?

I spotted the dairy section from afar. Several anxious masked-up shoppers had already lined up around it taking turns grabbing jugs, each more careful than the other not to come too close because of course we all really did have cooties this time. I sped up just as a woman took the last two gallons. Wanting nothing more than to tackle her to the ground and pull the gold from her, I knew that would be a problem if I did. Half of my list was now sold out. Then a man's voice from behind startled me and his words took extra time to register in my seething mind (also because who can really hear properly when they are speaking behind a mask?).

"Here, take this one." He put a gallon into my cart, smiled with his eyes, nodded, and walked away. What was happening in the world? What was it about today that was so...nice? Maybe the Zoom calls to mommy dearest had folks getting a remedial course on social interactions and good manners? Maybe.

On my way to the checkout line, I decided to make a quick stop for kale. Reaching up to grab a plastic bag for my leafy greens, I jumped back dropping the veggies, my heart thumping wildly at the sight before me. This was exactly how I'd pictured a gunman (or woman!)—shades, cap, hoodie, mask. But, I realized soon enough, this was no gunman, it was my own reflection in the mirrored panel of the kale section. I looked horrific. Yet, this look I had on, as monstrous and ghastly as it was, was welcomed by those around me only because I was not visibly Muslim. This hood and cap on my head were doing exactly the same job as the blush-colored fabric I had left at home, right alongside my thoughtfully curated garments, none of which were welcomed here.

All those times I had been mindful to not fit the stereotype of the "Muslim woman", my colors of choice being pastels, whites, creams, anything but black, even when my seriously-introverted, partially-goth self would opt for that out of comfort, none of it had mattered. Jeans and jean jackets, summer dresses, twirly skirts, whatever meant to fit in, I had tried. But I never will fit in. Rarely will people notice my choice of wardrobe; their focus will always be on my head robe.

This is America, the Land of the Free—free for whom exactly?

Dressing how I choose to is my free will and nobody's business. I refuse to blindly obey society's idiotic expectation that my body is their right, to be viewed and judged or even touched on demand. You too? Me too.

50 SHADES OF ATHLEISURE

by Kathryn Sadakierski

Every day, I am faced with a choice. A groundbreaking decision that will decide the trajectory of my day. Perhaps even my future. It is a complex, delicate process, answering this fundamental question of what set of pajamas I should wear to conduct business today. Babies have their Sleep N Play onesies and I have casual athleisure wear that is socially acceptable for wearing outside on the rare occasions when I step foot into the world beyond my place of self-quarantine, while also being comfortable enough for luxuriating at home in.

There are so many different kinds of groutfits, it is beyond comprehension! How do I possibly choose? Selecting different combinations of sweats is no joke, man. I mean, I've got to be on point for my daily walk to the mailbox. What would the neighbors think? Speaking of neighbors, even the people you think you know are unrecognizable nowadays. I'm seeing peoples' true colors since the hair dye at their roots is fading ever faster. Each day presents some new revelation of what someone really looks like. There are some things even Zoom backgrounds can't hide, like home self-haircuts gone wrong (somehow the bald stripe amidst layers of hair across the back center of his head didn't seem natural).

At this point, I seem to have forgotten what my hairdryer looks like; it's been so long since I used it. Hairspray? Forget it. My couch won't mind if I have a hair out of place. Professional blowouts? Psssh! You know how long it's been since my last haircut? Besides, the predominant quarantine trend is the Chewbacca look. That's just as well, since my home hair salon routine has been, to say the least, minimalist. These days have involved much more of a natural beauty regimen if you will. This is one time when the "before" photos are better than the "after" photos.

I'm not sure when the last time I wore makeup was. Then again, why wear makeup when your mask covers half of your face? There's no need! With social distancing, no one can examine my makeup-less face too closely anyway. But before you start thinking that my current state is totally disheveled, please, let me assure you of the most important thing: I'm still keeping my eyebrows in line! That level of upkeep is an achievement in these times, I tell you. With all of the eyebrow-raising headlines on the news every day, it's especially vital.

Masks are certainly a hot commodity now and no one is immune to this trend either. I've opted for a bandanna as my face covering, giving me the appearance of a germophobic outlaw from the Wild West whenever I step foot in the grocery store.

One can't help but miss dressing up for something besides a Zoom meeting, blissfully cozy as it is staying in fuzzy socks and slippers (every day is what the Danish would call a hygge day now). Hence, occasions are created to bring the extraordinary to each otherwise ordinary day blurring into the other. It's National Nacho Day? Oh, guess it's a great day to try on that dress you wore to your cousin's wedding years ago. Yes, even if your entrance into public society today consists of bringing out the trash. People will just think that you're about to attend an at-home prom; no worries! In these times, it seems like nothing is too unusual anymore. Expect the unexpected and all that.

Hey, when online shopping is the zeitgeist, why not buy some new dresses, even if I'm all dressed up with nowhere to go? Fashion, then, can be fun and personalized: wearing what you love, perhaps putting on some makeup just because it brings you joy, not to impress anyone.

Ah, here we are, arriving at the heart of the matter. When we think of the quarantine, we may think that this is an inopportune time for vanity. It has, after all, inspired rampant hair growth, the likes of which make no-shave November seem tame by comparison. With so much time spent indoors, when people do go outside, they are like moles emerging from belowground, seeing light for the first time, and blinking amazedly at the sun. In this time, though, there is an opportunity to move past insecurities, to embrace inner beauty. From this place of hardship can rise strength and serenity, the tenacity to keep moving forward.

Every day, we're learning new things about ourselves as we discover our creativity and resourcefulness, making the best of things (making a face mask from a cotton sheet and elastic hair ties, for one. Scrunchies always come in handy, when they're not getting lost at themed '80s parties or after yoga classes. Seriously, where do those things go?). Now, instead of focusing solely on appearances, we can measure the kindness and selflessness that people show, seeing the inner light shining from within. No bronzer needed for that glow!

THE UGLY STAGES OF QUARANTINE: FROM DUCK HEADS TO STRIPPER POLES

by Kristen Ferreira

Quarantine has been quite an odd time to say the least. Sometimes I am flying high and other times I cannot move from the couch. There have been a lot of phases. Let me highlight a few.

The teaching cat tricks phase. There was a solid two weeks where I honestly believed I could teach Cheddar how to jump in synchronicity to Van Halen's "Jump." I tried hard, incorporating toys and treats, and was often met with a complete dead stare. I wondered if rock was not his jam and did a song change to "Jump" by Kriss Kross. Cheddar then totally gave up and began napping an awful lot. So, I moved on to:

The walking/jogging phase. Now, I am no stranger to the streets, but I have been outside a whole lot more as of late. I am not the only one; sometimes I peer out the window and see the mass of people and wonder if they had ever heard of the great outdoors prior to the pandemic. It is like they finally had an epiphany that fresh air was an option. Truthfully, seeing these people doing people-y things is giving me more anxiety than the virus itself. In general, I can handle darting past them on the streets. I love that abruptly turning in the opposite direction when you see someone coming is now considered being courteous and not rude. That said, the running into people aspect of walking has led me to refer to my outdoor jaunts as "anxiety walks" on my to-do list.

The binge-watching stage. We've all done it. All I am going to say on the matter is to be cognizant of what you are watching in relation to the blanket in which you are snuggling. Weighted blankets are supposedly good for reducing stress and creating comfort. However, they must be used with caution. For instance, may I suggest not using one's weighted blanket while binging murder mysteries? Trying to lift the blanket to pee is eerily like what digging one's way out of a grave must feel like.

The ugly stage. I would like to forget this one. I swear I have turned into Jerry's girlfriend on the Seinfeld episode, *The Strike*. In the episode, his love interest looks either perfectly lovely or perfectly hideous, depending on the lights and the shadows. I have been going through a similar issue. Sometimes my hair is doing these gorgeous things, but my face is that of a teenage girl who has eaten nothing but greasy pizza. My breakouts got so bad at one point, I ordered a rubber duck head from Amazon to cover my face and therefore, zits. It has come in handy for both Zoom meetings and for sending boys sexy photos.

The shopping phase. This has been a long and expensive one that includes me buying products ranging from sneakers, meal delivery subscriptions, and exercise equipment.

To begin, sneakers. All of a sudden, I am Googling and buying sneakers as if I am my brother back in 1998. I've purchased a bunch of sneakers and now I'm afraid to wear them for fear they will soil. The result is multiple pairs of tennis shoes, mainly sitting in my kitchen, just so I can wave to them as I walk by.

The meal delivery subscription started off well and good except for a few minor details. One, I somehow created two accounts and therefore was receiving double the shipments as well as getting billed twice. Second, I would then forget what day it was, resulting in the meals sitting in their boxes for far too long. Third, I have irritable bowel syndrome so having complete meals consisting of semi-thawed meats and excessive beans certainly did not help that situation.

Buying exercise equipment is half sensible, but there is also a "WTF were you smoking?" aspect to these purchases as well. First, I bought an exercise bike from Amazon and used gift cards towards the purchase, so I do not feel too bad about that, especially since it ended up only costing me $100. Of course, this does beg the question as to how good the bike could possibly be, and furthermore, it does require assembly, and I truthfully do not see that going well.

The real kicker of a purchase however occurred after some excessive day drinking. Somehow that morning I had awakened convinced that I needed to embody my best self, which of course meant purchasing an exotic dancer pole. (I should perhaps mention that I drank a few rum and Cokes, which I hadn't had in about 15 years.) While I was too ill to move my actual body, I was unfortunately not sick enough to avoid scrounging Amazon for the best deal on stripper poles. I was thrilled when I found one for a mere $225 and clicked on "buy now" because I was that pumped.

Thankfully. I had the common sense to review my purchase many hours later when my head was able to move again. Ladies and gentlemen, what I had thought to have been the stripper pole of my dreams really ended up being a pole to assist elderly people with getting out of the shower. Fortunately, I was able to cancel the order, though in retrospect, such a pole may have really come in handy. Also, not for nothing, I feel the padded parts of the pole would have limited the amount of bruising that may have happened if I had in fact used it as its intended purpose. Those couple of times that I took exotic dance class left me quite black and blue.

Between day drinking, elderly stripper poles, and sneakers that taunt me, quarantine has sure had its share of downs. Slowly but surely, however, the world will start to open up again. While this sounds like a positive thing, I will miss hiding in my duck head, spending time with my cat, and of course, avoiding people.

FASHION & MAKE-UP TIPS FOR GOING BACK TO THE OFFICE

by Ellie Connor

We've all gotten used to working from home, so much that transitioning back to normal office work-wear may be harder than holding back a cough in a crowded supermarket. Sure, being in close proximity to annoying (and potentially feverish) colleagues fills you with some dread, but let's be honest—the *real* nightmare is the thought of switching back to power suits after months of comfy sweaters and food-stained pajamas. But fear not! Read these top tips to make your work-from-home style work in the office.

1) Make your robe a statement piece in the boardroom.

Turning off your Zoom camera to hide your robe isn't an option back in the office. But why hide it? Work it! All you need to make your robe a "look" are some big hoop earrings, a fancy belt, and a bold leopard print scarf – just make sure to shake off the crumbs before that big meeting with the stakeholders.

Let's be real, we've seen more ridiculous looks at New York Fashion Week, and what better way to convey that you're ready to get back to work than with a statement piece that screams "Ahh! I'm having a mental breakdown!" Top tip: make sure your belt color coordinates with your pink and fluffy robe to really nail that profesh look. Bonus points if it also matches that wine stain from 2018 you couldn't get out.

2) Get a makeover to match your webcam filters.

Quarantine has made some of us reliant on using webcam filters to look like we just came off the red carpet, even while recycling last night's make-up. But for face-to-face interaction in the office, 1.5-meter distance isn't going to be enough to hide your sleep-smudged eyeliner and mascara stains. The solution? Wake up an extra three hours early to get your make-up to look as good as camera filters. It'll be totally worth it so that your boss doesn't ask why you look tired or sick!

Although make sure to go easy on the fake tan – after all, we all know you haven't been on holiday. If you want to take it a step further, buy some bunny ears from your local costume store so you can look like the cute animal filter we all think makes us look better for some reason. Sadly, this won't hide your crooked nose in real life, so you'll just have to save up for a nose job like the rest of us.

3) No legwear? No problem!

Thanks to lockdown, wearing trousers at work seems like a thing of the past. But when you get back to the office, you can't stay behind your desk all day or turn off your camera when you stand up. So what to do? It's simple – grow out your leg hair. Honestly, the longer the better. With the new air-conditioning system in the office, you'll be wanting to aim for the "could be mistaken for Sasquatch" look.

Just think of those glorious 10 minutes of extra sleep you'll get in the morning – which, let's face it, you're gonna need if you're waking up three hours early to do your make-up (see tip #2). If you really want to rock the leg hair look, try adding decorations to spice things up: googly eyes, anyone? You can also add some body paint to show off your creativity, but just be sure not to get it in the wrong places, or you'll be so itchy down there COVID-19 might be the least of your worries.

4) Use your facemask to hide your true feelings.

When Max from finance tells you to smile more, you can't put him on mute and blame it on an internet problem. The solution? Use your facemask to hide your true emotions! When someone makes a sexist joke during lunch, you can scowl and swear all you like behind a facemask—just remember to keep your voice down; you can't put yourself on mute now either.

Make sure you have a facemask for every day of the week—not for health reasons, but because quarantine was just one giant blur and you still have no actual clue what day it is (no, it's not Friday). Warning: you have to be extra alert about hiding your feelings if you're PMS-ing, as your crazy rage eyes might give away that you're *not totally psyched* to have to train the new intern. Our suggestion? Wear a black ski mask that pretty much covers your whole face. What better way to introduce a bright young mind to the company than looking like a '90s bank robber?

Top tip: If you've always dreamed of being a vigilante, now is the time! Every time you put on your facemask, use your best Batman voice and be the hero we all need to find out who keeps stealing food from the shared fridge.

5) Unwashed hair for the fifth day in a row? Wear a hat!

Forget the rule of no hats indoors—we've gone through a pandemic, old fashion(ed) rules have gone out the window. Make grease the new in-vogue look! After all, hats were made for can't-be-bothered-to-wash-your-hair days. However, your choice of hat is *crucial* – you need something that covers all your greasy roots, so a beret is a big no-no unless paired with a highly distracting fake French accent. A cowboy hat is possible, but only with matching boots and attitude—yelling "Yeehaw!" every time someone mentions revenue or profit margins should do the trick.

If your hair is too greasy to be salvaged by a normal hat, we recommend you try an astronaut helmet—if your boss questions you about it, just shout "new data privacy laws!" before quickly running off. Don't forget, you can always pair the unwashed hair look with a fancy up-do; not only will you look fancy AF in meetings, but it'll make it easier to hide your snacks in.

6) Want people to keep their distance? Shower less!

Sometimes that 1.5 meter/ 6-foot distance rule seems like a blessing, especially when that co-worker of yours really insists on having garlic for lunch. But if your colleagues need that little bit of extra encouragement to social distance, then maybe continuing that no-shower streak you had at home isn't the worst idea. Let others know of your no-wash status by having a sign on your cubicle wall saying how long it's been since your last shower. Even better, send out a daily email blast encouraging others to join you in your no-shower mission—you can claim it's for the environment, but you'll know the truth. Trust me, people will definitely leave you in peace after this. Besides, did I mention you can get ten minutes extra sleep?

7) Finally, if you want that 25% raise, don't shave the quarantine moustache.

You might be mistaken for a man!

There you have it! Going back to the office doesn't have to be that different from working from home. Just remember: When you get back to work, people can smell what special liquids you put in your cup. So if you're going to get day drunk, at least get yourself a chic "water" bottle that matches your best power suit.

Family and Parenting

THE QUARANTINE QUICKIE: HOW ONE MOM COPED WITH COVID-19 LOCKDOWN IN SPAIN

by Linda Freund

Showers and haircuts were the first things to go. Then came our waist-lines. Finally, our wits. For 44 days, mother, father, and son were confined to our pencil-shaped apartment in Barcelona. No outdoor exercise. No walks. Only essential dashes to the market or pharmacy.

Spain's COVID-19 lockdown was one of the strictest in the world. Our long days indoors took on the status of mystery meat in the school cafeteria – best left unexplained. Most of it involved dodging bad breath and sharp elbows as we juggled work and homeschooling. There was illness on our doorsteps, in our neighborhoods, and amongst our friends. It was heartbreaking, but we managed to stay healthy. Really, we suffered only the luxury of cabin fever...

But quarantine sex? Yeah, that was an afterthought for these exhausted parents. Our agenda was already packed:

We longed for the spring of Barcelona's sidewalk tiles under our feet. Or, at the very least, a reason to put on shoes. Each day, our son-turned-cat stared at the sunspots from the open window (his daily vitamin D dose). The outdoor people watched clouds. The Freunds? At this point, we watched whatever you put in front of us.

One fine morning, my husband and I stared at spilled coffee grounds. "It's kind of...beautiful," I said. We sighed in appreciation.

"It looks like a cheetah," my husband replied. (It looked nothing like a cheetah.)

We were coping. And, from where I stood, we were doing a proper job of it.

Everything changed one winter day (or was it spring?). It was like the hand of the almighty himself had entered our Zoom call…only to take our neighbors off mute! The results were carnal. The mystery meat had hit the grill.

The *vecinos* (neighbors) you see, had rekindled their romance under lockdown. And by rekindled, I mean the humpy-bumpies behind paper-thin walls. I'm all for their ingenuity in passing the time, but it's impossible to teach your 6-year-old multiplication between pleading moans, let alone field a journalism call with a priest (true story).

Question: What's one grunt times one spank plus an "Oh yeaaaah!?"

Answer: Loud. That's what it is. Really freaking loud.

Added bonus: There would be no noise complaints. The main participant, after all, was our own landlord's daughter. The birds, the bees, and our neighbors.

"Why are you making that face," our youngster asked me in the minutes following their climax.

"Oh. Uh, mommy just ate something sour."

Translation: Our little Pythagoras had no idea what that sound was. Actually, no reaction whatsoever. For all he knew it was a stray cat in distress. Instead, he scribbled away, counting numbers with chubby fingers.

After the neighbors popped their quarantine cherry, the habit took on a daily cadence. Always lunchtime and always loud. Another line item on our family's timetable.

8 a.m.	Wake Up.
9 a.m.	Shower (optional). Breakfast.
9:30 a.m.	Get son online for English class. Work.
10:45 a.m.	Get son online for Math class. Work.
12:00 p.m.	Listen to neighbors have sex.
12:30 p.m.	Lunch.

At first, my husband and I stared at each other awkwardly from across the living room. Our heads poked out from behind our respective laptops.

After a blur of days, we replaced eye contact with a verbal sigh. The weirdness had turned to jealousy—how dare they enjoy their lockdown suffering! Why aren't we making passionate love in the living room at all hours? Oh, that's right. We're parents.

Truth be told, I could have made myself more available to my fellow inmate. Sure, I showered once a week and yes, my hair was so greasy you could fry potatoes in it. But I still had my youth. Then again, my husband wasn't much better. When his hair grows, it grows up. As in straight up. He was the spitting image of a treasure troll minus the neon.

One day during the matinee session, my husband tilted his head. Was that a wink? Yes, I think he winked.

We'd been playing the social distance card long before it was trendy. As working parents, intimacy is already a poker game from recoil to embrace. One minute, you desire alone time. The next, you're touching each other's no-no spots as a passing greeting.

It was 12 p.m. under lockdown. The moans rang out with Swiss accuracy. Did this woman never get her period? I noticed my husband's remote workstation had moved a little closer. One couch cushion closer, to be precise.

Visions of quarantine sex danced in my head—as did the logistics. Could we steal some time between our son's late bedtime and our Netflix lullabies?

Most couples had experienced a sort of freeze-frame amid COVID-19 shutdowns. According to a recent Monmouth University poll: amid the stress and anxiety, the vast majority of partners reported their relationship in terms of "Groundhog Day." Their arguments were the same. Their sex life? Also the same.

Our neighbors were clearly the anomaly here. What about us?

The next day my husband wore a shirt with a collar. My goodness. In lockdown that's the equivalent of peacock plumage. I noticed.

Two days later (maybe three), my husband winked again. It was definitely a wink. I smiled without teeth. Later that day, I trimmed my hair with blunt scissors over the bathroom sink, followed by a battery of bobby pins to hide the results. I looked good.

Another day began. The neighbors' cries rose like the mighty sun. My husband's minty-fresh breath hit my face. He quickly took my hand and guided me to the bedroom. It was happening.

Laundry piles pushed off the bed. Shirt dangling from one arm. A wet kiss. The feel of water on a parched tongue. Then, a doorknob rattle.

"Mommy..."

"Crap." Shirt jammed on just in time.

Our son stood at the door, his eyes made even wider by the iPad's glow.

"Do you wanna see what I made?"

"Oh yes, honey, I do. But right now Mama and Papa are working on a Zoom call."

My husband laughed. I gave him the look.

"Okay," our little boy said.

Was the mood ruined? Please, oh quarantine Gods, don't let the mood be ruined.

"Don't interrupt us unless it's urgent."

"Okay, Mommy."

More laughs. Door closed. Chair jammed under the knob. Day-pajamas off. Then, our bodies touched. The feeling was pure heat.

Touch was not on the schedule.

My lips tightened. Outside, an accidental brush with a stranger could be lethal. But an inside touch, a sterile invitation to feel skin? That was beauty—a reminder of the life we were all fighting so hard to preserve.

Forget toilet paper and flour, touch had become the true scarce resource of the pandemic. Something we longed for to plug the void, but also a thing to be feared.

I traced my husband's shoulder. He stroked my cheek. Then, our quickie commenced. And for the first time in a long time, I felt whole. Skin-to-skin for five minutes max. Maybe 10.

Silence and speed, after all, were everything lest we corrupt our son's childhood. Because when parents have sex, let alone mid-day quarantine sex, it's always quiet, with the mic on mute.

Immediately after, we squeezed our day-pajamas back on and opened the bedroom door. It was 12:30 p.m. after all. Time for lunch.

"Tomorrow, I'll wear a tie," my husband said.

BOUGIE "BAAJI[1]": LESSONS IN INTERSECTIONALITY FROM THE LOCKDOWN

by Sarah Shamim

"Humaari jesi achi families waalon ko thori hoga Corona." People from "good" families like ours will never get Corona.

I recently heard this from a friend who was quoting a distant relative, *burger aunty*, who justified having elaborate *desi*[2] wedding functions and *Eid* holiday parties because apparently viruses don't affect rich people.

Now if you're wondering what a "burger aunty" is, worry not because I'm here to educate you about them. Typically in Pakistan, an "aunty" is a woman your mom's age-ish (who you may or may not be related to) who thinks she is entitled to having opinions about your appearance and credentials and loudly voicing said opinions, which is always delightful. It always helps when they ask me to put on more weight while I'm just trying to *flex my grades, please just let me*.

But burger aunties are truly my problematic faves. "Burger" is a very vast term but it's mostly used to describe the rich, elite, *bougie* class of Pakistan. Think of them as a Pakistani version of Karens. Thanks to social media and icons such as *Swineryy* on Instagram and *Naik Parveen*

---

[1] Urdu for older sister, also used by house help to address female bosses
[2] Of South Asian/Indian subcontinental descent

Syndrome on Facebook, satire surrounding burger aunties is now on the rise, so hopefully I won't be in trouble after this is published.

Alhamdulillah[3], I don't have many conversations with the bourgeoisie, but the handful of rich friends I have make me believe that not all burgers are actually classist. However, a good handful of them really are, and aunties and uncles are a bullet-proof-vest if self-awareness and social reform are bullets, for the lack of a less violent analogy.

Back to the point, some burger uncles and aunties have been having quite a lot of social gatherings during times of the virus. These gatherings have a lot to do with talking about whatever rich people talk about (I wouldn't know), and a lot of "drawing room talk," which is a word I use to describe *desi* uncles sharing their "wonderful insight" about politics.

It's pretty cute how, when a lot of families gather, the men sit in the drawing rooms, slurping chai and talking shit about women while the women are in a separate room or in the kitchen. This is not limited to burger families since I have seen it in my very own non-burger family. Gross, I know. However, since I'm still young and ever so quirky, I make rounds in both the uncle and aunty sections to get *all* the tea and gossip, and somehow, get away with it.

Now, *desi* uncles have garnered quite the reputation for trying to out-mansplain each other, which is always hilarious to watch from far away. Who needs to spend a thousand rupees on a Netflix subscription when you have organic, all natural, home-grown entertainment?

Their tragic misinformation is just as hilarious. Their confidence when they regurgitate factually incorrect information from chain WhatsApp messages out loud is something I can only aspire to have. Fact-checking is for losers and poor people anyway!

Many uncles relished in a moment of flourishing ego when COVID-19 broke out in our country. The fact that the virus hit Pakistan a mere week before our women's march was quite the cherry on top for them. Misogynistic uncles who previously lacked any good comebacks except of course "ShUT UP LibeRl weSTern girl" to anyone who dared speak against honor killing and acid attacks, now realized it would be very witty to say that this virus is a punishment for feminists who do not believe that women should stay inside their homes and cover their faces.

It was very confusing and ironic because men also have to stay at home

---

[3] By the grace of God.

and cover their faces because of the virus. Unlike some misogynistic *jaanus*[4], the virus does not only attack women. Also, burger people are typically big on talking only in English and not even buying from local brands, so it just doesn't sit right that they think gender equality is a western concept.

But also, these are the same burger uncles who continue to have gatherings and think that the virus is a joke. The cognitive dissonance jumped out, or something?

There is one thing for sure: a lot of bougie people here are not terrified of the virus and are okay with the fact that every single person in the country will contract it eventually, which freaks me out because not all of us have a 20-storey bungalow where every member of the family can self-isolate with their 100 adult coloring books. Not all of us have actual *hazmat* suits like the ones the soldiers in *Stranger Things* had to help to serve us luxurious meals to our doorstep.

Also, saying all of us will eventually contract the virus is totally not insensitive to the entire working class that would barely be able to survive. Nope. Haha.

I will admit though, sometimes I just feel like I'm projecting my own guilt that I'm quarantining comfortably when I'm overly critical of the privileged classes during the lockdown, but then I see upper-class classist uncles and aunties get away with literally everything and I hate saying this, it makes me feel better about my own behavior.

---

[4] Urdu for sweethearts.

FINALLY, THE PERFECT TIME TO HAVE A BABY

by Naomi Fitter

Until recently, I thought there was no right time to have a baby. My mentors had pointed out the pros of waiting (from having a better knowledge of yourself to being past certain career milestones) while my doctors showed me alarming charts (although the thing I always wonder most is: who gave the okay to call 35-year-old women "geriatric"?!). Doing my own mental calculus, I sometimes wondered if the best time for me to have had a baby was actually in high school.

But now...never has there been a time when I have fewer reasons to leave the house. My work hours have never been more flexible. My wardrobe has never been more stretchy! Finally, could it be...the perfect time to have a baby?

I hear you—you're worried about job security. You wonder if your local hospital will have capacity during the present pandemic. The world is warming and on fire and you're reluctant to bring a child into it. No matter your placement on the no-baby-to-baby spectrum, I've got a pitch for you.

Before Pregnancy

- You're bored; you're cooped up; and you're continually noticing how loudly your partner chews. Focusing on making a baby can alleviate at least some of this stir craziness.
- Nowadays, you might be feeling empty inside. Well, pregnancy

is the literal antithesis of emptiness!

- If you're like me, you bought 10 bags of frozen spinach at the start of the pandemic and then realized you never really cook with frozen spinach. Could it be...finally a time for all that folic acid?

During Pregnancy

- Video chats neither give away your baby bump nor convey the slight scent of morning sickness on your breath. Or that you're eating for two.
- No one will give you unsolicited advice about your pregnancy.
- You don't have to buy maternity clothes. I mean, who wears clothes anymore, am I right?
- No shame for your daily cup of coffee.
- No stuck-on wedding rings. No one's watching to see if you wear your wedding ring in the first place! I'm a programmer who can't wear her ring while typing, anyway. Let's face it, it's not getting much mileage to begin with.
- Nobody will touch your belly. Nobody will touch you at all. You're alone. So, so alone.
- When you run out of Netflix shows, you and your partner will be able to play "Is the baby kicking?" for hours on end.
- Instead of wondering, "Am I having a boy or a girl?", you'll get to wonder exciting new things like "When does the Phase 2 reopening start?" and "Is there toilet paper at Safeway?" or "Is humanity done for?"
- You won't have to go through the trouble of hosting a gender reveal party, because you won't be able to get a doctor's appointment to learn the sex of the baby in the first place. And along the way, you won't have to explain to your family members that gender reveals are dumb because gender is a social construct.
- Your partner is also stuck at home. You know what that means? Foot rubs. Anytime.
- If you go out, you can claim your belly is just depression weight from social isolation.
- The only baby shower you'll need to host is the monthly shower you're currently taking during quarantine.

A Few for My Female Faculty in STEM Fields

- Everyone's already getting a one-year extension on their tenure clock...no one will ever ask you about that one-year gap on your CV.
- No one will be weird about the pregnancy because no one will know.
- Need to tinkle or vomit? Your 2.5 baths at home offer three times as many toilets as the single women's bathroom stall at your workplace.
- No need to use maternity leave because no one will notice the difference in your quarantine work output anyway.
- Your potential graduate students won't pick non-pregnant/male advisors over you.

After Pregnancy

- It'll be easy to get plenty of bedrest. These days, you don't even have to leave bed...
- No one will judge you for nursing.
- No one will see your varicose veins, mainly because if you're anything like me, you haven't shaved so far during quarantine...
- Bringing your child to work still won't be smiled upon, but at least there's no alternative now.
- Any room that's not at least 6 feet across is yours for the taking as a lactation room.
- Whether it's during your third trimester or after the baby arrives, you can't travel anyway.
- Your postpartum depression and anxiety will be well disguised by natural reactions to the modern state of the world.
- Your whole family will never be short on milk.

SLEEPING WITH THE CAT

by Meg Riley

On day 52 of isolation, I realize that my cat and I have become an un-happily married couple. She is an 8-year-old Calico named Turnip who has big green eyes, a large, fluffy belly, and the brazen personality of a retired Hollywood diva. I am a single, 27-year-old woman on the brink of a nervous breakdown who, these days, spends her time counting the minutes until it's acceptable to have a glass of wine. Sometimes it's 5 p.m. Sometimes it's noon.

Quarantine has not been a walk in the park. Literally, because I ha-ven't been outside my apartment besides to buy cookie dough at the gro-cery store and figuratively because I am currently three weeks removed from the death of a childhood friend and a former lover. Still, things could be worse. I have my job and my apartment. I have my health. However, despite all of these complications and minor miracles, most days all I can think about is how horny I am. Teenage boy horny, con-sumed with fantasies about being ravaged in the hallway of my five-floor walkup by the pizza delivery man.

Sadly, the only one I'm sharing my bed with is Turnip. Every night she slinks into my room from whatever corner of the apartment she's been hiding in all evening, my door creaking ominously in the dark to alert me to her arrival. I slide over to make room for her, and she curls up next to me against the empty left side pillow where, many moons ago, a human male's head once rested. Of course, that was a different lifetime; one in which the sex market was saturated with supply and demand, and the possibility of spending the night with someone was always at the tips of my fingers. Since quarantine began, I am lucky if I get a single match on a dating app, let alone an actual conversation. The idea of human touch is an obsolete luxury.

The cat and I settle into our nightly routine like old lovers. I toss and turn, trying to get into a comfortable position. Turnip grumbles and huffs, often beginning to snore loudly. If I'm fortunate enough, she'll treat me to the gentle slurping noise of her licking her own asshole. In the dark, it sounds like someone giving the world's sloppiest blowjob.

During the days, we quarrel. We're not used to being home together for such long stretches of time. She gets irritated and hostile when I disrupt her morning nap routine by moving my laptop or kicking her out of my room and she shrieks at me and I roll my eyes. We do this dance once an hour for the rest of the day. When I'm working my now remote 9-to-5 gig, she waits until I'm about to press "send" on an email, sneaking up next to me and deliberately pressing her chubby little paws onto the keyboard. "Talk soon" turns into "Talk soonxcv4``/" and I yell at her. She shrieks at me and the cycle begins once again.

Privacy with Turnip is nonexistent. She cries when I take a shower. She cries when I use the toilet. She has an uncanny sense for knowing when I'm about to masturbate, and at the exact moment when I am poised and ready under the covers, she will leap onto the bed and settle her doughy body onto my midsection, purring smugly against my pubic bone. When I finally convince her to relocate, she sits at my feet and looks me directly in the eye as the vibrator starts up, glaring at me like a disapproving partner who's been left out of the fun. I close my eyes and try to imagine I am somewhere else, anywhere else with a hot man and a door that locks with a single, solitary moment of peace and quiet.

My friends envy our companionship the way I envy anyone who's quarantining with their boyfriend. "I wish I had a cat," they complain. "Turnip is such an angel."

Sure, it's nice to have a creature for comfort, but I'd rather be cuddled up inside with someone who is capable of fucking me. Preferably someone who can also cook and carry on a conversation, instead of what I am stuck with: the small, furry monster who tortures me each night with a saliva symphony that's too grotesque for even a porn audio and an endless demand for my unwavering attention.

Of course, it's not all bad. Like any couple, we have our ups and downs. Inevitably, after we fight, she comes wandering back to me, chirping a hello, nuzzling her head against my leg or blessing my arm with a sandpaper kiss. It's sweet.

"Come on," I tell her, gesturing to where I'm sitting, and she climbs into my lap like she owns it, nestling in with a satisfying plop. All is forgiven.

Since quarantine began, I've been having trouble sleeping through the night. Sometimes, I'll wake up from a restless dream and see her big eyes watching me in the dark, blinking slowly at me from the left side pillow.

Occasionally, she'll reach out a paw and gently touch my face or my hand. Or she'll get up and readjust herself to fit perfectly in the crook of my body, making herself the little spoon, and I think: This is nice. Her soft fur. Her gentle breathing. Certainly more comfortable and more comforting than a man's sweaty ball sack sticking to the back of my thigh or his heavy arm draped awkwardly across my chest.

Don't get me wrong; I'm not trading in men for good. I pray that every day of isolation might bring me closer to my next orgasm at the hands of another person. I'd even take a dick pic from the right sender. Some days, I get so desperate that I think I would gladly throw Turnip in the Gowanus Canal and light her surprisingly hefty body on fire if it meant I could feel a man's hands on me.

But as the days get longer and lonelier, I must confess: the cat is a welcome companion. I talk to her when I'm making dinner or re-organizing my bookshelves for the third time in a week. She never reminds me to shave my legs or points out that I've gained a few pounds. When I am laid low by life's uncertain circumstances, she curls up next to me without prompting, humming contentedly, pressing her wet nose against my leg.

And sometimes, when I find myself dancing in the kitchen, cradling Turnip in my arms singing, "You're my dirty little muffin baby" in her face, I am forced to admit that ultimately, I'm not really a guys' girl after all. I'm more of a cat lady.

BEE CALM AND CARRY ON

by Daien Guo

It was our 70th walk of the coronavirus. 35 days total of quarantine. With young kids, two walks a day is the minimum...for sanity and suicide-prevention.

Daycare and school had closed abruptly in March. Now we were outside on a balmy and idyllic afternoon in late April. Nature gave us a global pandemic but also one of the dreamiest springs in recent memory. Or was this the first time I possessed the leisure to admire it?

My five-year-old was already sick of walks. Or maybe he wasn't.

The secret to parenthood is: do not to try too hard to divine the inner lives of your children, especially during a pandemic. Nothing good can come from it. I blithely ignored what my kids might be feeling.

This was easy because I had spent a lifetime ignoring my own anxieties. With all this practice in emotional constipation, I was preparing for The Big One. And when COVID-19 hit, I was smug in my cold composure. I felt nothing. Really, nothing at all. I would not indulge in self-pity. I got through the day. I am competent. I am calm.

Still, for my kids, a walk was better than staying in the house watching their 5th hour of TV for the day or licking the mildew off the grout in the bathroom shower—not that they do that or anything.

We made it around the block.

"I want to go hooommmme..."

"No, let's keep going," my husband urged.

"I'm tired."

Kids are very tired around 6:30 p.m., but they recharge like a magical

Tesla and are at their frightening full strength by 9:30 p.m.

"Let's go to the community garden. Let's show Mommy the bees."

With playgrounds and parks closed in the early weeks of the pandemic, people with kids just congregated in other hilariously inappropriate locations: parking lots with shards of shattered glass on the asphalt, neglected grass fields not part of any official park system, alleyways behind ghostly empty commercial buildings—basically places where the high school delinquents used to gather to smoke weed. (I wonder where those teenagers went—perhaps they dutifully sheltered at home now, frightened into retreat by the invasion of drooling large-headed toddlers and mothers in leggings on their turf.)

Add to the list: community gardens with beehives.

"Bees? Why would we go look at bees?" I wondered aloud, a remark that proved to be prescient.

At the community garden across the street, my son showed me a beehive that has a picture of Winnie the Pooh on it. The warm air smelled pungent and mulchy. I examined the composting system behind the storage shed. I wondered if I should start composting.

The first scream sliced through the air like a cleaver made of Japanese steel.

"AARRGHHHHHHHHH!!! A bee stung me! AHHH. AHHH. AHHH. AHHHH."

The later screams were rhythmic and jarring, like the repetitive siren of a police car from a 1960s French movie. My five-year-old son stood frozen, clutching his hand, his large brown eyes tearing up and showing the betrayal and hurt of an innocent who just now realized all the friendly animal creatures he read about in books, like bears, lions, tigers—and bees—are in fact wild animals who can and will hurt him. Who writes these books anyway? People who have never actually been around animals?

My husband ran to our son to swat the bee away. The screaming continued. I immediately looked for my one-year-old, who was standing right next to the beehive. I sprinted over to pick him up and started running toward our home.

I feel nothing. I get through the day. I keep calm…except there was a loud buzzing I couldn't ignore. So loud. So close. Too close. There was a bee in my hair, just behind my ears, just above my neck? I have never been stung by a bee before. Does it hurt?

I was suddenly very very scared. The theoretical catastrophe of a global pandemic was eclipsed by the immediacy of the danger buzzing centimeters from my scalp.

Holding my child with one arm, maintaining my brisk pace, I used my other hand to try to untangle my hair and swat the bee out. This was before my quarantine self-haircut, so my hair was long, dense and full of damaged split ends. The bee didn't care. He seemed to like it in there.

BUZZZZZZZZ... BUZZZZZZZZZZ... BUZZZZZZZ...

I had to get this bee out. I couldn't walk home with this bee. I put my toddler down and I dropped to my knees on the ground, using both hands to comb through my hair. Will the bee sting my neck, or my scalp, or my hands? I heard my other son still crying and screaming behind me.

"Adam!" I yelled at my husband.

"Are you okay?"

"I have a bee in my hair! I have a bee in my hair!"

Now my one-year-old sensed something in the universe was awry. He looked at his older brother, who was still howling with pain. He looked at his mommy, who was kneeling on the ground, faceless, her head just a ball of unruly black hair. Then he promptly joined in the chorus and erupted into a tearful wail.

In the odd time of social distancing, a few other people in the community garden observed the drama from afar. I couldn't tell if they were horrified or amused. This was not exactly Shakespeare in the Park, but the bar for live entertainment during COVID-19 was very low.

My husband was now by my side, his fingers in my hair. He later told me the bee was burrowing deeper and deeper, as if trying to dig into my scalp, perhaps mistaking my head for an oversized peony.

"Okay, okay, it's out!"

I rose to my feet and picked up my child. We started walking home, all a bit dazed. My older son was still softly whimpering, clutching his hand, tears streaming down his face.

I would consult Dr. Google as soon as we get home. I would watch Youtube videos on how to give myself a haircut. I would cook dinner. I get through the day. I am competent. I am calm.

THE NOW TIMES

by Adina Gillett

SCHOOL. For me, the word evokes images of classrooms, hallways, bursting Trapper Keepers, lockers stuffed with stinky gym uniforms and worn books, bleachers, jocks in letterman jackets cavorting with cheerleaders, banners advertising socially threatening dances, and cafeterias full of pizza sliced in squares and life or death seating selections. Until this past March, a similar montage of images (albeit updated from my '80s version replete with shoulder pads and concho belts) probably came to mind for most of us when invoking the word SCHOOL.

But then, everything changed. No, I'm not talking about "The Good Place" ending and leaving a massive hole in our collective hearts (but while we're talking about it, seriously, c'mon. I'm still not okay). I'm talking about the second-worst scourge to attack the world since January 20, 2017: Coronavirus, heretofore to be referred to as The Now Times.

The Now Times looks like many things: empty streets; frenzied supermarkets that simmer simultaneously with the energy of "We're all in this together, dear community" and "Stay the fuck away from me, you germ-ridden commie!" Ghost towns that used to be shopping centers, shuttered theaters, and no more getting caught behind the school bus' red flashing lights and stern metal arm blocking the road while we guzzle our coffee in our cars anxious to Mario Cart to the freeway so we can slam the brakes and inch forward for an hour.

You know. The Before Times.

School is officially out, and homeschooling is taking place in many different ways around the world. Some schools have launched into synchronous learning, where the teachers are live and on video, as are the kids, and it is a true virtual classroom. Some schools are sending home worksheets and videos for the kids to do. And some schools are simply closed, as their students don't have the resources such as home computers or Wi-Fi, to do much work at all. But in all cases, one thing is consistent—education has changed.

Around here, there are some clear signs of this change. Whereas my daughter once put on clothes and left the house for school, she now wears pajamas and Sasquatch slippers. Her hair (once considered an integral part of negotiating the minefield that is the social pecking order) displays in a devil-may-care rat's nest that sings *This Is Me* from *The Greatest Showman*. Her high school changed its grading policy to pass/fail in an effort to minimize the kids' stress (a decision I applaud) and in recognition that most colleges with likely call this semester a Drew Carey and say "It's all made up and points don't matter," because, let's face it: in The Now Times, they don't.

Sure, she needs to keep up with her biochemistry, art history, and precalculus because that work will continue when The Now Times becomes The New Times. In The New Times, she might be at some bar's trivia night at some point and will be able to summon the word "chloroplast" out of the brain vault where she keeps the majority of the schooling that's only useful for bar trivia.

For now, though, I have learned that as a parent, my once passionate rigor for cheerleading her studious efforts has been replaced by, what's the word? Oh yeah—"don't give a shit." I'm finding it really difficult to stress over her Spanish quiz performance or that she forgot a letter in the Ideal Gas Law when an actual pandemic is ravaging the world and the outside has become *Jumanji* as the animals are clueing into the fact that we are AWOL. I don't know about you folks, but my education priorities have changed.

My first Amazon purchase when The Now Times arrived was a knife-throwing kit because my kids are going to know how to throw knives in The Now Times. Our bows and arrows are coming out of attic retirement. My once lukewarm efforts at gardening have become a Defcon 3 drive fueled by the idea that those carrots and potatoes (which last year I so callously took for granted) could now save us from the barren battleground that is Safeway. I'm thanking my own foresight of six years ago for giving my son a lockpicking set for Hanukkah, as we are all now becoming very adept at jimmying open padlocks.

This stuff is the skill set I'm looking to grow in my kids and myself in The Now Times. The kid doesn't want to do her World History assignment on Napoleon? Fine, do it later—let's learn how to trap rabbits (one never knows).

Is that math assignment getting you down? Do it later—we're getting low on butter and may not be able to get more so let's churn some (one never knows).

Feeling restless? Let's cut each other's hair.

Let's bake. Paint. Go biking.

And my personal favorite? An online hostage negotiation course, because who wouldn't want to know that shit? Say it with me: one never knows.

None of this is to say that I don't think my kids' schooling is important anymore. It is absolutely providing a semblance of routine and familiarity that is critical to maintaining a sense of stability, hope, and future focus.

School will continue. This is temporary. Earth is recovering. There will be The New Times. I can't be grateful enough to the heroic teachers that revamped an entire career of how to teach in basically a weekend and still show up for our kids while managing their own dismantled home lives.

Seriously. The teachers. I want them to have this entire line. Thank you.

I recently read an article called *The Secret of Immigrant Genius* by Eric Weiner, that espouses a theory of why immigrants are responsible for a preponderance of Nobel Prizes, patents, and global awards, despite being a minority of the population. It is most often chalked up to how immigrants need grit to survive in a new land, so immigrants work harder than non-immigrants. But the article instead proposes a concept called Schema Violation, a condition that "…occurs when our world is turned upside-down, when temporal and spatial cues are off-kilter." When immigrants have everything familiar and routine is taken away, they are then forced to view their new land at a different angle than those of us who occupy it already. They see things differently, from an outsider's perspective, and this encourages genius—previously unseen ways of seeing things.

I'd say a pandemic qualifies as a Schema Violation.

Perhaps, as we wade through The Now Times, we recognize and accept that there will never be The Before Times again, and acting like things will go back to "normal" does not serve us. Who knows when we'll need those stinky gym uniforms again or have that tepid square pizza in the quagmire of the cafeteria.

While I desperately hope my son gets to return to college and my daughter someday brushes her hair again, I'm also pretty impressed with how well they can now pick locks, and The New Times might have a lot of doors. One never knows.

A THEATRICAL SCENE BETWEEN MY 3-YEAR-OLD AND ME: BY AN UNEMPLOYED PLAYWRIGHT

by Laura Wheatman Hill

The theatres have closed but the drama doesn't stop. Here lies an actual exchange between LAURA, a 30-something mother, dressed in shapeless sweats, and WESLEY, three-and-three-quarters-old, in very cute monster pajamas.

Set in a modern, but dirty kitchen. Plates from last night are still in the sink. Legos and crumbs adorn the floors. Excessive collages are stuck to the cabinets, an attempt at keeping the toddler busy during the rainy days. Morning sun streams through the blinds.

WESLEY: (sitting on the floor) I want a wolipop.
LAURA: It is 7 a.m. You cannot have a lollipop. You need to eat some breakfast.
WESLEY: I peed on the potty!
LAURA: I know you did. I'm very proud of you.
WESLEY: I get a pwize.
LAURA: I did say that didn't I? You can have a prize after lunch. It's too early for candy.
WESLEY: Just one?
LAURA: Your father is a dentist. You can't have a lollipop before breakfast!

WESLEY: If you don't give me one —
LAURA: You don't get to threaten me!
WESLEY: If you don't give me one —
LAURA: Don't.
WESLEY: I'm gonna (whispers) swear.
LAURA: Kids can't swear.
WESLEY: I'm gonna swear!
LAURA: Grown-ups can swear. And vote. And drive.
WESLEY: WOLIPOP!
LAURA: NO!
WESLEY: (SENSELESS SCREAMS!)
LAURA: (YELLING OVER HIM) THE REST OF THE FAMILY IS SLEEPING! YOU'RE BEING TOO LOUD! YOU ARE GOING TO NEED TO TAKE A TIME OUT! JUST EAT SOME CHEERIOS!
WESLEY: (big deep breath. Then...) YOU STUPID FUCK!
LAURA: WHAT?!
WESLEY: YOU STUPID —
LAURA: NO! Don't say it again. You can't swear.
WESLEY: YOU —
LAURA: STOP! Holy fucking shit! STOP! Go to your room (reaches for his hand).
WESLEY: (boneless and crumpled) No no no no no no don't make me go to my ROOOOOOOOM!
LAURA: (forcibly carries the boy to his room) Go! WESLEY: DON'T LOCK IT!
LAURA: Take a deep breath!
WESLEY: (full voice) I CANNOT!
LAURA: When you're willing to talk to me like a civilized human, I will let you out!
WESLEY: WOLIPOP!
LAURA: When you're willing to have breakfast, I'll let you out. (she shuts the door. Wesley continues to scream for quite some time. Eventually, he quiets. She opens the door) Are you ready? (she reaches for him)
WESLEY: (holding his hand up) No love.
LAURA: No love? Fine. How about some Cheerios?
WESLEY: (nods) Then wolipop?

LAURA: Later, yeah.

WESLEY: (holds up his hand) I touched my blood vessels.

LAURA: Your what?

WESLEY: Dada says I have blood vessels in my penis and not a bone.

LAURA: Well. Okay.

WESLEY: When I poop, it feels like snakes.

LAURA: Did you poop?

WESLEY: When I poop, it feels like snakes coming out of my BUTT.

LAURA: Can I change you now?

WESLEY: Slimy snakes.

LAURA: K.

WESLEY: Poop is slime.

LAURA: I guess so. Wesley? No more swearing. Grown-ups can swear. Not kids.

WESLEY: Grown-ups can say fuck.

LAURA: Don't say it.

BLACKOUT

SURVIVING QUICKSAND IN THE AGE OF QUARANTINE

by Laura Iodice

I'm living proof that it's possible to stay afloat while immersed in quick-sand. All you have to do is to avoid both struggling and sinking and surrender instead.

My unfortunate entrapment began before the current pandemic rendered everyone adrift. Before we uprooted my 89-year-old, cognitively impaired mother from her downstate New York apartment and moved her into our upstate home. Before her ailing 90-year-old husband was admitted to a New Rochelle nursing home to receive hospice care. Yes, you read the location correctly. New Rochelle, the epicenter of downstate New York's coronavirus epidemic, in a nursing home placed on lockdown.

Undeterred, my mother's husband made nightly attempts to escape. He'd slide from his bed, search for his street clothes, then ring the nurse's station and insist that they call his wife to pick him up, even though a.) she no longer drives; b.) his efforts necessitated that he drag along an oxygen tank while wearing a diaper and using a self-propelling wheelchair c.) their marriage has always been as volatile as Chernobyl.

COVID-19, too, was a festering mess just waiting to erupt, until the two inadvertently collided, resulting in the current quagmire where mother, my husband, and I now spend our days and nights interminably together; where my mother wakes up each day not remembering why she's here or what happened to her husband and every day feels like a bizarre rendition of *Groundhog Day*, a movie that I loathe as much as I would being trapped in an elevator with Bill Murray's character—or with my mother.

And I'm not the only one who's struggling. Our rescue pup now shares her space with my mom's purebred who's taken over all the doggie beds scattered throughout the house, hoards all the doggie toys, drinks and eats from our dog's dish instead of her own, and piddles with impunity. Oh, and she also snarls and snaps unpredictably at my mother. My mother's response?

"It's not Holly's fault! She's just letting me know that she doesn't want me to pet her." Or: "She's a good dog. She just likes to let me know who's boss."

How do you explain to someone incapable of remembering where she now resides that her dog struggles with a severe personality disorder and desperately needs treatment, but doggy therapists are a low priority while on lockdown during a pandemic?

More tragically, how do you enable her to comprehend that her ailing husband passed away while in hospice care? In an effort to cushion the daily blow of reminding her, our family physician increased her Alzheimer's medication dosage, but instead of the desired effect, Mom went from egotistical to egomaniacal overnight. The other day, she stalked into the kitchen while I was preparing her lunch, pointed to her hair and declared, "My roots are showing! I need to get to a beauty parlor today!" At nearly 90, you think she'd be able to forego her leather pants and red ringlets, but...

"Mom," I patiently reply. "We're currently under 'stay at home' orders. The hairdressers are closed."

"Well, doesn't the supermarket carry hair color? You can color it for me!"

Note to drowning self: "Add Clairol Ruby Red to the shopping list. P.S.: Call the doctor and ask her to prescribe additional meds for mom."

Of course, this won't resolve Mom's hearing issue. Not only does she forget what I said five minutes ago. She can't hear what I'm saying as I say it.

"Would you like to go for a walk?" I ask, in an effort to distract her from relentlessly repeating the same questions over and over again.

"You want me to get you a fork? Why don't YOU get the fork?"

And finally, when Mom comprehends that her husband, whom she used to refer to as "That worthless slacker," has passed away, she assails me with revisionist history:

"Poor Sam. He had such a good heart."

I nod in agreement, keeping my lips securely in place.

An hour later, "Laurie, I have a question. Did Sam die?"

"Yes, Mom. I'm so sorry."

She looks puzzled, then replies. "How could this happen? It was so sudden!" She sighs, then: "Only the good die young."

This, because she can't remember that he was over 90, had COPD, heart disease, and diabetes. This, even though their relationship was beyond contentious on a good day. Still, I shrug my shoulders in commiseration.

"I want to go home," she whines, while I coax her to eat "breakfast" at noon, since she's still in her pajamas. "Mom, you ARE home!" I cheerily respond.

"I mean my apartment! Who gave your brother permission to clean it out?" she cries, even though she'd overseen the entire process, via Facetime.

Desperate for respite, I call both the doctor and the vet. Mom and her dog are now on anti-depressants, but this hasn't stopped either one of them from alternately snapping, growling and whimpering at their caretakers.

Or fixating, like she does when brooding about the leopard make-up case she'd hidden years ago in a shoebox inside her apartment closet. Who hides her remaining savings, a not-so meager $15,000, in a leopard make-up case buried in one of about 50 shoe boxes on the closet floor? My mother, Imelda Marcos' doppelganger!

And who squanders over $150,000 on a lifetime of extravagant travel, exorbitant purchasing, and prohibitive overspending, but remarkably, manages to squirrel away a pittance, just in case? Who but my mother would now decide, in the middle of a pandemic when she has no memory, no hearing, no vision, and no husband, that now is the "just in case" time she's been preparing for?

"What's left in the shoebox? Are you sure your brother hasn't spent the money?"

"Mom," I reply. "Jerry has the shoebox in a safe place. All the money's there, so let's not worry about it." Not worry? Who am I kidding? I'm the *Queen of Worry* under ordinary circumstances, and now, I'm straddling quicksand while in quarantine! Yet still, there's a certain peace in owning my perplexity.

Let's be real: we are living in unprecedented times when even a neighborhood walk can become a cautionary tale and even the experts have no answers.

And neither do I. But I do know this. I've found joy in articulating my experiences, even while struggling to adapt to them. Perhaps the answer truly is to relinquish control, to surrender, and to make our peace with drifting in place. Even with a dog and a mother snarling at us repeatedly.

BREASTFEEDING TIPS WITH MR. SLOTH

by Sara Savusa

The weather is turning warmer in the Midwest. Sweet, sweet summer is just around the corner. Here in Chicago, our shelter in place order to help flatten the curve of global pandemic COVID-19 went into effect on March 21, 2020. People are getting antsy. The temptation to go sip a cocktail out on a patio with friends is tortuous. Under different circumstances I would be on my bike in a heartbeat, headed to Lake Michigan with a book. But these days, I am stuck at home and loving it. I am Mayor Lori Lightfoot's biggest fan. Her meme game is strong; let's stay home a few more months! Oh wait, I will be. Why? Because I'm pregnant in quarantine, baby!

By day, I managed a baby boutique; by night, I performed and directed improv and live theatre in Chicago. If I'm lucky, I'd book a few film gigs here and there. I am really proud I didn't let this pregnancy slow me down. With the help of blazers, oversized jumpsuits, and blanket scarves, I continued my usual life pace, no questions asked. Never having time to go home midday, I packed a bag with clothes, hair and make-up supplies, and food to last me until midnight. I booked more with my little secret bébé than I have since moving here in 2013. Must be the glow.

But by the time March 21st rolled around, I was 21 weeks and starting to feel the slowdown. My belly was clearly showing, and I struggled to pick out comfortable and cute outfits.

Putting compression socks on while pregnant is cardio. Assume the figure skating sit spin position. Pulling up on the sock while navigating around the mountain in your abdomen really gets the heart pumping, like wrestling a boa constrictor. March 22nd, I burned all my bras and pants. (Just kidding, those buddies are expensive.)

I am extremely fortunate to continue working my boutique job from home, especially since my husband was furloughed from his job. Working retail from home entails a super professional human (me) helping customers with their orders in a vintage 1995 University of Hawai`i t-shirt and full coverage cotton underwear bouncing on a birthing ball. As the weeks progress, my boobs and belly expand, bringing with that the downpour of sweat, and I am able to tuck washcloths under each boob without judgment. Imagine if I was still going into work? I anticipated working, like most modern women, up to my due date. The misery! Like most performers right now, I continue to perform via Zoom, sitting in comfort atop my birthing ball. The joy!

The craziest part of all of this are doctor appointments during this quarantine. Pregnancy means a lot of doctor visits, especially towards the end. The week prior to the shelter in place order, Husband could accompany me to the momentous 20-week anatomy scan, which I am extremely thankful for because I almost passed out from being flat on my back too long.

Two fun facts:

1. Lying flat on your back while pregnant blocks the flow of blood in your vena cava.

2. If you pass out at an appointment, they are required by law to call you an ambulance. Turns out medical personnel aren't your best friend who will call you an Uber to save money.

Literally the next day, medical facilities across the U.S. said no guests or visitors can accompany patients to appointments. My appointments promptly switched to telehealth, which made me worry if a hacker would put me up on *GirlsGoneGyno*. Thankfully no exams were performed via Zoom, just verbal check-ins. They wrote me a prescription for a blood pressure cuff for home use and instructed me on how to measure my growing belly with a tape measure. If *Call the Midwife* is casting, I'm ready.

I hope Zoom only lives in the confines of this pandemic. It currently serves as the gatekeeper to every facet of my outside life, personal and professional, including baby classes. My favorite moments of the six-week program include the instructor having us play charades with birthing vocabulary and practice birthing positions. Every other couple muted their computers and turned off their cameras, but Husband and I turned into a Vaudeville act, forcing our instructor to watch us. At the end of each position we smiled, held our pose, and went "Huh???"

I used a stuffed animal to practice breastfeeding positions and techniques; his name is Mr. Sloth. I see trauma in poor Mr. Sloth's eyes. He can accompany my kid to therapy someday.

Now I'm in the home stretch and my appointments are back in person at the office, but it is different. I go alone: screened and temperature taken at the door before entering. Riding the elevator with strangers causes me mild panic; silver lining, no one is making conversation. In the waiting room, there are no more than three of us, spaced out, and all wearing masks. My favorite nurse wears a face shield like she plays for the Chicago Blackhawks. She mentally prepped me for the big baby eviction day: my husband and I will both be tested for COVID-19 prior to being admitted. If the husband tests positive, my Samwise Gamgee will be sent home, and I, Frodo, continue the journey alone. If I test positive, I will have to labor in a mask. Keep in mind, this is just my practice. Many hospitals and birthing centers across the United States require laboring parents to wear masks regardless. So everyone complaining about wearing a dinky cloth mask while grocery shopping, suck it up, buttercup.

Our original plans to have family come help us those first few weeks after the birth are obliterated. We have no family within reasonable driving distance, nor do we have a place they could affordably quarantine for two weeks prior to seeing us. The more I read about how challenging the first two weeks after birth are, I wonder if we'll end up like the old couple on *Titanic*, spooning in bed to our deaths, while the new baby screams in the crib.

The scariest part of this entire pandemic is there is so much unknown. No one knows how long this will last or when a vaccine will be available. Babies have no immune system; it is possible we will be hunkered down hermits for the long haul. So be on the lookout for my Zoom one-woman show: Breastfeeding Tips with Mr. Sloth.

PANDEMIC SYNDROME RETIREMENT

by Patricia Florio

My husband fell out of bed in the middle of the night. I hadn't seen someone do that since my daughter rolled off her "big girl" bed in 1979.

"What the hell happened?" I ask, as I try pulling his arm upward, hoping to get him off the floor.

I couldn't budge him. I was too weak, or he was too heavy for me to handle by myself.

"Should I call an ambulance?"

"No, no, please don't. I'm not having a heart attack. It's a vertigo attack. I've been dealing with this for about two months. I didn't think it would get so bad."

All I could think of was Alfred Hitchcock's movie, *Vertigo*, as visions of crisscrossed wires created a picture in my head.

He lay on the floor flat on his back and seemed content enough to close his eyes.

"Please shut the light," he utters, "I can't take the brightness and, goddamn it, call Dr. Beal," he says, really angry with me.

I felt terrible for him, but who told him to get so darn heavy that I couldn't move him up onto the bed?

"Ralph, we're in a pandemic, there's not going to be a doctor on call tonight or any time soon."

"Just leave me here," he says.

So, I did.

Later that morning, Ralph maneuvers his hands up the mattress and pushes and pulls on the sheet until he gets himself on the bed. "Get my phone," he demands in a pretty irritated tone.

As a dutiful wife, I retrieve his phone. I'll admit I want to smack him with it, but I don't. I hand it to him all nice and calm. I leave the room because I don't want to see a grown man cry.

When I look in the next time, he's fallen asleep, no pillow under his head. I call my daughter and tell her about her father and what had happened in the middle of the night.

"Mom, you should have taken him to the hospital."

I wasn't taking anybody's guff, especially from someone I had pushed out through a small slot down below. Did she not know how quickly the pandemic was spreading and that people were dying all over the world? If she had taken any news she watched seriously, then she wouldn't have asked her mother to sacrifice her life for her father's.

I have not gone over the edge yet and I prepare and bring Ralph an English Muffin—his favorite morning food before he takes his pills. But I see he's trying to pull off his PJs and he's not having any luck. I rest the dish on our dresser and lay him back gently on the bed, pull off the legs slowly, not to cause any additional movement to his already nausea-ridden brain.

Of course, I am aware that the off-kilter feeling he's going through is an inner-ear infection, and if he could get some relief by sleeping or keeping his stomach full, he might be able to kick this thing himself. It's like having a bout of seasickness.

"Get my pants and help me get them on. Dr. Beal has an ENT guy who's going to see me this afternoon."

"How are you getting there?" I ask.

"You're driving me."

I was being put at risk—couldn't the man just sleep it off?

After I help him put his sweatpants on, I sit next to him on the bed and he folds the muffin in half and stuffs it in his mouth.

Masks on, like two bandits going to rob a bank, I help Ralph into the van, buckle him in. I get on the driver's side and I drive an hour to the ENT doctor's office, only to find out that I can't go inside with my husband. Nor can I use their bathroom. "Patients only" rule!

A masked nurse comes to our car. I roll down the window on his side. She takes Ralph's temperature; our new normal and she escorts him into the doctor's office.

I wait in the car.

A half-hour goes by.

Then an hour.

I'm gone crazy by this time. Plus, I have to pee. Bad. An hour and a half later, Ralph walks towards our van with a smile on his face and gets on the passenger side. I'm wondering what could be so funny. Just two hours ago, you would have thought he was at death's door.

Between his index finger and thumb, Ralph holds up University of Hawai`i an olive pit? a bug? Something dark and alarming looking.

"You know what this is?" he asks holding the pit—bug—ball of goo from his ear.

"I don't think I want to know," I say.

"A Q-tip," he says. One of those Dollar Store brands—cheap, only a dollar for a whole box. God knows how long it's been in there," he adds.

Oh, God, this is my husband. He used to be so debonair, a snappy dresser in a dark suit and tie. His every day going to work costume, hob-knobbing with judges and lawyers.

This is retirement? Shoot me now!

TIPS FROM ITALY: HOW TO SURVIVE THE COVID-19 LOCKDOWN WITH A TEENAGER

by Katherine Wilson

International Women's Day this year came on a Sunday, the day before Italy declared a national lockdown. "Let's celebrate our rights and look optimistically towards the future!" we declared. And then, after less than 24 hours, guess what? We're going to be at home with our children for the next two weeks and probably longer!

Whether they are toddlers or teenagers, our kids in lock-down need to be managed. And they are most likely going to be managed by us, the mamas. In these first weeks of lockdown, I have realized the importance of *sdrammatizzare* – **that wonderful Italian art of sucking the drama out of something that is truly dramatic.** It's the art of keeping a smile on your face when confronted with catastrophe. Italy, with its history of wars and plagues and economic disasters, could never have survived without it. When life is rosy, it's fine to be dramatic. When there is a crisis, it is essential to keep a sense of humor and irony.

If you are not able to *sdrammatizzare*, I'm afraid, you might not survive a lockdown with teenagers. So, I've compiled a few do's and don'ts to help us make it through the next few weeks.

DON'T: Walk into your kids' rooms and speak.
There is no way to know whether your kids are "in class" when "class" is in your home. You will see them in front of a screen, but then again they

are always in front of a screen. Yesterday I entered my son's room in pajamas (a positive aspect of the lockdown-elastic-waisted pajamas at noon are perfectly acceptable!). Handing him some orange juice, I used a term of endearment that hasn't come out of my mouth for years. How could I have known he was in Latin class? His teacher and peers did not see a domestic goddess fighting to keep her family healthy, but a fuzzy, shuffling crazy lady whose roots had grown out. Be warned.

DO: Let go of "screen time" worries.
Biology class becomes Instagram which becomes TikTok which becomes Houseparty. Accept it. Global technology gave this virus the possibility to travel at the speed of light, and it also gave us Netflix. Nobody is expecting you to entertain/stimulate/engage your children when there is a global pandemic afoot.

DON'T: Obsess over cleaning.
I'm sorry to be the one to break it to you, but you do not live with homo sapiens. You live with pigs. The sooner you own this, the better. Would you be bitter or passive-aggressive with cute little piglets? Of course not. Let go of the possibility of a clean house: it's not going to happen.

DO: Cook things that take forever.
Remember those recipes that said soak the beans for four hours or sit overnight in the fridge? The ones you knew you'd never have time to make? It's lockdown! You have endless time to let things simmer, rise, and soak. Your kids, despite the fact that they are not engaged in any physical activity outside the house, are ravenous. Always. (Make sure they scrub the pots—they've got the time!)

DON'T: Try to keep siblings from fighting.
Space, WiFi, remote controls, phones: they will have it out over anything and everything. Don't revisit Siblings Without Rivalry lectures, just tune them out. Beats headphones are great!

DO: Take off your watch and *nap.
Timekeeping as we know it has only been around since the Industrial Revolution. It was instituted for train travel and factory production. Since there is no travel or production in the time of COVID-19, we can

go back to the early nineteenth century, when people ate when they were hungry and slept when they were sleepy. Basta! Enough! with the tyranny of the clock! (*Nap does not refer to dozing on the couch, but to the full lights-off-under-the-covers deal. You need to wake up with pillow lines streaking your cheeks and drool out of the corners of your mouth. If you don't nap during lockdown, when will you ever nap?)

DON'T: Let the kids take the dog or the garbage out.
That is your privilege. There are very few legally sanctioned outings, and you get them. Last night my husband and I were elbowing each other to get to the stinky plastic trash bag: one of the symbols of lockdown "leave." Proud to report I made it first, and also clocked in four walks with the dog.

DO: Hide your phone chargers.
Your teenagers eat them. Or maybe, in addition to smartphones, they plug in other things—things you don't want to know about. Whatever it is, there is a bizarre phenomenon where your phone is regularly at 7%, even though you're at home all day, every day. You need to stash the cords or they will disappear.

DON'T: Expect anyone in the house to answer a landline.
As an experiment, I let the phone ring 13 times this morning. Not only did my teenagers not answer it, they didn't even cock their heads like curious dogs. I believe that evolution has eliminated that frequency from their range of hearing.

DO: Facetime high school friends you haven't talked to in ages.
Our kids are interacting online constantly with their peers, but those of us born in the last millennium tend to be passive: Instead of scrolling through Facebook or texting/emailing a friend, call your peeps! You don't need to make an appointment—they're at home like you are. Chances are they'll be ecstatic to hear from and see you. Even with your lockdown hair situation.

DON'T: Read COVID-19 updates on the news.
This thing can become a sick reality show—addictive and horrifying. It can encourage you to spin out apocalyptic scenarios. We know that all

we can do is wash our hands, take care of our health, and stay at home. Our grandparents were asked to go far away and die for their country. Stay at home? Doable.

Work and School

FACT-CHECKING:
THE TRUTH WILL SET YOU FREE... UNTIL IT WON'T

by Fernanda Estrada Argumedo

It's been hours and I'm involved in a vicious fight in my family's group chat. One of my aunts already called me "communist" and misgendered me. Some uncles and cousins are taking sides and my mom already attacked someone with the "And you are...?" weapon. After I set this scene, you'll probably wonder how I got here and who I am, to which I'll turn my head, stare at the camera and say: This is me. My name is Fernanda and I was a fact checker during the outbreak of COVID-19.

For eight months, I lived, slept, dreamt and ate COVID-19 lies. I read the classics: "COVID-19 doesn't exist", "Can't we just drink bleach to kill it?", "COVID-19 PCR tests can damage your brain" and "vaccines have microchips to control us". But, if you're in México, as I am, you know those classics also include "healthcare workers say you have COVID-19 to hospitalize you and steal the fluid from your knees", for instance. And nope, I'm not even lying, that fake article went *big*.

For eight months, that was my everyday: interviewing doctors, healthcare workers, authorities, and chemists; intensive conspiracy theory readings, reverse image searches and infinite approaches to understanding scientific documents. All of it, with the sole purpose of explaining a bunch of people, *why* you cannot cure COVID-19 with lime tea.

Don't get me wrong, I liked my job and I humbly believe it is one of the most important and necessary activities during a pandemic. But, after repeating myself and the words of respectable doctors so many times for eight months...I was proud, yet tired (just as an empowered, independent woman is these days).

This exhaustion leads me back to the scene in the family chat.

My aunt had sent a video assuring that chlorine dioxide could prevent and cure COVID-19 (spoiler alert: it doesn't and it's harmful, please don't drink that shit), to which I answered with an infinite amount of medical papers and fact-checking articles refuting it. And that was the spark that lit my own bonfire.

It was then when I understood the source of my tiredness. And perhaps I discovered the loophole in the system: Shouting truths at people is not enough. Shaking medical papers in front of someone's face doesn't really work that well.

The thing is, ever since 2016, thinking about fake news inevitably brings us back to politics: Whether a certain president keeps lying publicly (you'll never know if I'm talking about US or Mexico) or conspiracy theorists assure the COVID-19 crisis is a *plandemic*, a machiavellian and complex strategy by powerful countries or individuals who want to rule the world and control humanity (spoiler again: it's not).

And while "the personal is political," I believe the politics on this topic have had its fair share of exploration. It is what my aunt's very personal mind was up to that intrigued me. And misunderstanding it was tiring me.

So, once again I'll pause the real-time family chat scene and break the fourth wall for a brief version of Fake News 101:

"Disinformation is information that is false and deliberately created to harm a person, social group, organization, or country. You know, the political stuff, for example. Misinformation is information that is false but was not created or shared with the intention of causing harm."

And that is the key to it. My aunt was not sharing this video with fake information to harm me or the other members of the chat, she was sending it because she cared. And, of course, caring is no valid justification not to verify one's shared messages, but understanding why she did it is clue enough to know why throwing academic PDFs at her face meant nothing.

There's an evident problem in the education system and the media and our politics if we cannot tell if the information we share because we care is full of lies. But still, us, the ones who have the privileges to actually notice, we sometimes forget about caring. We roll our eyes and scroll past the recipe to cure COVID-19 with garlic that our uncle sent.

Yes, corporations and governments need to be held to task when it comes to disinformation. But disinformation and misinformation need to be addressed from a number of fronts. Maybe if we paid closer attention and understood that some of the misinformation comes from people that care about us and want us not to get COVID-19, we'd be more patient to explain (and sure, later share *all* of the med papers).

It actually doesn't take much from us, but care.

LOST IN TRANSLATION

by Brooke Stanicki

"MA'AM, WERE YOU DOING ANYTHING BEFORE YOU FELL?" I asked my patient, a stout 98-year-old whose medications were written down on the back of a Dunkin Donuts' receipt.

"What? I am not selling this purse!" she replied, clutching her knock-off bag.

Elderly women couldn't hear me before the pandemic. For some reason, despite the fact that I was often screaming at them, my EMS partner always had to translate on my behalf. My non-scientific hypothesis was that it was something about the pitch of my voice—I produced an incorrect resonance that only impacted older women. Or maybe they just don't like me.

The pandemic was my worst nightmare. Not because I was scared of contracting COVID-19 at the time. Honestly, at work, a respiratory disease wasn't high on my list of concerns. A few weeks prior, I was clocked right in the face after reviving an overdose victim.

"You ruined my high!" my patient shouted as he rose from the dead to swing like he found the spirit of Rocky, punching me right in the eye. My boyfriend said it looked fine, but my gross, swollen, bluish-green eye socket and I knew he was lying.

COVID-19 itself didn't scare me. It was the fact that no elderly woman was going to hear me through the new personal protective equipment protocol—an N-95 respirator and a surgical mask.

"DO YOU HAVE ANY CHEST PAIN?" I asked through my layers of masks.

"No, I don't think it's going to rain" my patient, an 80-year-old former mail carrier calmly responded, pondering the weather report.

After a long 12-hour night shift, I got home, my face slightly dented from my masks, my voice hoarse from the screaming. My family heard me speak and immediately assumed I had COVID-19.

"Hey, did you want any cereal?" I croaked, offering my sister the box. She sat at the head of the table, as far away from me as possible.

"No, you can have that box. You touched it and stuff!" she responded, leaning away from me, as if COVID-19 couldn't reach her if she just increased her radius by a few inches.

"Whatever." I said, over-filling my cereal bowl, just because I could.

A few days later, back at work, I asked my partner for advice.

"The key is, you have to enunciate your words. Really throw your words at the patients. Pretend like the masks aren't even there," she coached me. "Here, let's practice, I'm your patient."

"OK MA'AM, HOW LONG HAVE YOU BEEN INCONTINENT?" I screamed at her.

She shoved my shoulder with her purple-gloved hand. "Go social distance yourself," she snarled, but couldn't hide her growing grin.

The next call we got, I took my partner's words to heart. I imagined throwing my words across the room. I did a little vocal warm up as we arrived on scene, chatting to myself before starting to speak with the patient, a 74-year-old female who had fainted and hit her head. To my surprise, my primary assessment went off without a hitch. When I spoke, she responded appropriately. I thought I had finally cracked the code to talking to elderly female patients. I was silently ecstatic as we lifted her onto the stretcher and wheeled her into the ambulance.

Once she was safely secured in the back, I remembered that I had forgotten one question.

"DO YOU HAVE ANY ALLERGIES?" I asked, throwing my words, enunciating as clear as I could into my N-95.

"Yes, I love Applebee's! The ladies from the Bridge Club love the chicken, but it's too spicy for me," she responded.

I sighed. I hadn't cracked the code just yet.

By the next shift, the personal protective equipment protocol had changed again—full HazMat suit and face shield to protect the N-95. I knew I was doomed. I winced when my radio squawked its normal tones.

"85-year-old female, difficulty breathing," the dispatcher reported.

My HazMat suit crinkled with every step. And my face shield kept lightly hitting my nose. As usual, when I started my assessment, my patient couldn't hear me. My partner repeated what I was saying as I recorded a set of vital signs. We moved her into the ambulance, and I strapped her in before sitting down.

"HOW ARE YOU FEELING WITH THE OXYGEN ON?" I asked her, adjusting the nasal cannula tucked into her nostrils.

"I'm sorry dear, I cannot seem to hear you," she responded.

Sick and tired of not being heard, sick and tired of COVID-19, I let my words slip for just a moment.

"DO YOU LIKE MY OUTFIT?" I asked, sarcastically, thinking she would never hear me.

"It is a bit scary," she responded, "doesn't do anything for your figure."

I don't know if she heard it or not, but I laughed all the way to the hospital.

ZOOMING IN, TUNING OUT

by Anndee Hochman

Write down one question you have about poetry, I instruct the kids.

The "kids" are a palette of tiny faces, 4th-graders from an elementary school in Princeton, New Jersey, staring at me from the screen of my MacBook Air. I'm a teaching artist, and the PTO of this school is paying me to virtually "visit" the kids' classrooms—which is to say, their kitchens and dining room tables and frankly disheveled bedrooms—once a week for a month, to guide them in writing poetry.

This means I have to get dressed.

It also means that, for three hours each Monday, I have to toggle between my typed-out lesson plans, the Zoom platform with its "share screen" and "gallery view" options, the clip of soft jazz I want the kids to hear while they write and the fetid, crumpled junk heap that is *My Brain on Quarantine*.

When my daughter was learning to count, she would recite: "fourteen, fifteen...*nexteen*." That's how life feels in the time of Coronavirus: Nexthour, nextday, nextweek. It's Someday in the month of Awful. I use a mindfulness app each morning in an effort to find equanimity, and I'm keeping a journal—three sentences a night, a low, achievable bar—because, without it, my short-term memory dissolves like soap.

The 4th-graders force me to be present. Some flutter their actual hands; some tap the yellow splayed-fingers icon on their screens. But their questions are urgent and real.

What is the longest poem in the world?

How do I let the reader know the theme of my poem without saying it right out? What makes a poem a poem?

Nineteen faces, each smaller than a quarter, lock eyes with me. "Let's wait a few weeks," I hedge. "Maybe then we'll be a little closer to an answer."

In the first class, the teacher gives emphatic instructions: microphones off, cameras on, don't wander away from the screen, Ms. Anndee doesn't want to see pictures of SpongeBob while you go get a snack.

But now it's 1 p.m. I haven't eaten or peed or moved from my ergonomic chair in hours and I'm knocking on the virtual door of classroom number three for nine minutes while frantically emailing the assistant teacher on my cell phone.

By the time she figures out the technical glitch and lets me in, the "classroom" is anarchy: kids sprawling on their beds, bouncing in their chairs. One boy takes extravagant licks from what looks like a lemon popsicle; another crunches carrot spears inches from his laptop's microphone. A girl tugs the cowl neck of her sweater up to her eyebrows.

They don't have notebooks. Or pencils. Adult arms wave in and out of the screen. Kids vanish, and suddenly I am looking at images of polar bears, rainbows and Kermit the frog. Where did Nicky go? What about Xen Le? Rohan, are you coming back?

In the contrived world of Zoom, it's easy to forget that I'm not speaking to an assemblage of children, each seated in a little box, but to 19 different locations at the same time. Am I teaching? Are we learning? Should I have taken down the poster hanging over my bookshelves, a souvenir from the ACT UP era, that shows three couples (two of them queer) engaged in playful lip-lock, with the slogan: "Kissing Doesn't Kill; Greed and Indifference Do"?

I show the kids my mascot, a small stuffed bear from Barnard, where my daughter goes to school. Went to school. Still goes to school, I think, if college means paying $27,000 a semester to take classes on Dangerous Art while perched in one's childhood bedroom, eating Goldfish crackers and wearing sweats.

I hold up my amethyst rock, a gift from my dad, and ask the kids, between now and next week, to find an object that helps them feel creative. Then I cue up the music and watch as they scramble for paper.

Astonishingly, they write. Well, most of them do. Some chat, forgetting to mute their microphones, or jump up in search of more snacks. Is that child waving, or just scratching? I'm looking at someone's carpet, someone else's half-closed closet door. The boy in the top left square is about to somersault off his bed.

I'm also staring, uncomfortably, at my own face: thick brows, dry lips, and crowded bottom teeth, despite three miserable years of braces tightened weekly by the orthodontist who was later convicted as a pedophile. Is it worth a new round of orthodontia, at the age of 57? Would my insurance cover that?

I reach for coffee. Is it okay if the kids see me take a swig? It's not like I'm guzzling bourbon in the middle of the day (though that has occurred to me). Anyway, they can't see inside my cup. My stomach growls. That popsicle looks delicious.

We have five minutes left. "You know how, at the movies—you remember movies, right?" I tell them. "How do you get previews of the coming attractions? Let's hear one-line previews of these poems."

"Any questions?"

"Ms. Anndee, what is your net worth?"

Who asked that? The kid who looks as though he hasn't combed his hair since pre-COVID-19? The one who declared, "Poems don't have to make sense"? The one who's still incommunicado inside the ribbed neck of her sweater?

My net worth?

Aren't we all asking some version of that, these days? I'm not talking about the nose-dive of our investments, but some deeper, existential measure, like, what is the cost I exact on the planet for existing? How much stuff do I really need? What am I giving back to the world, if I spend half the day in the same clothes I slept in, venturing outside only to tromp through the woods or procure more Greek yogurt and dish soap from Trader Joe's?

There is a beat of silence. The teacher calls names. They read:

I'm from city lights.

I'm from a place high up and far away.

I'm from teachers and preachers, gamers and explainers.

Whoa.

What is the net worth of any human being? Do you subtract quirks from assets to get the answer? Or self-absorption from good intentions? All I know is, a child's poetry just added something to the cosmic balance sheet.

What makes a poem a poem? That, exactly—the way words can swivel your gaze toward the horizon of possibility.

Before I click "Leave meeting," I remind the kids to have a week of discovery and surprise, of safety and peace. Then I wave. With my real hand.

WELCOME TO VIRTUAL HELL:
NURSING SCHOOL IN THE AGE OF COVID-19

by Alexandra Nicole Benson

Looking back on my life, it seems as though I was always predestined to become a nurse. As a child, I took care of sick and incapacitated stuffed animals (a lot of them didn't make it), as a preteen, I watched every season of *Grey's Anatomy* because well, someone had to do it. And as a teenager, I blossomed in my knowledge of anatomy and physiology (I did well in the classroom too *wink, wink.* Just kidding, I was terrified of boys). I even volunteered at the very hospital I am looking into for future residency programs.

It wasn't until I took one of those highly accurate and completely underrated career tests in high school that I realized: "Hey, I think I'd make an alright nurse" (or teacher or plumber. Okay, it wasn't that accurate), so I went with it! Upon graduating from high school, I received a nursing scholarship which got the ball rolling on my education. A few years and one public health degree later, I am in my second to last quarter of nursing.

As a nursing student, pre-COVID-19, I loved inserting NG tubes into mannequins, taking vital signs on unwilling participants, giving insulin injections into slabs of silicone, and priming IV tubing. I also occasionally liked to pretend I knew how to read EKG strips, give unsolicited advice on random ailments, and even dabbled in arterial blood gas interpretation. But who doesn't?! Ask me about that time I saved someone's life with these skills (I didn't).

My last clinical was in a maternity ward where my fellow classmates and I experienced the "amazing miracle of childbirth". Well, we were supposed to, but technically only half of my group got to see a live birth, myself NOT included. I was among the group who, instead, watched the same video every 14-year-old was scarred from and only very briefly scared into abstinence by in high school. Thank you, American education system! You know, the film from the '90s featuring a woman with beads of sweat rolling down her face, squeezing her ever-so supportive and slightly regretful partner's hand, with a close up of her legs in stirrups as she's giving birth to her beautiful, 8 lb. 6 oz., now 20-something, bundle of joy. I frequently wonder where these people are now and how they're coping with life.

I imagine the kid is amusing at parties—"Hey, remember that video we watched in Filer's 9th-grade health class? Yep, that was my mom! No, I never really got over it. Yeah, I still see my childhood therapist every Thursday...her name's Jan if you want her card."

Everything about my first year and a half of nursing was intense, but I loved it, even the dreaded on-campus tests. Looking back, I realize how fortunate I was to even have onsite experiences. I was so blissfully unaware as I walked out of my last clinical that I would never again have in-hospital experience as a nursing student. Why, you may ask? Allow me to elaborate.

I am a nursing student *in the age of COVID-19*.

Gone are the days in which nursing students get valuable in-hospital experience, and bring on the days of virtual simulation so students like me can still graduate in August! Woo hoo!

Look out, ailing citizens and healthcare communities around the world, a fresh batch of virtual floor nurses are graduating soon and coming to a clinic near you! We may not know our way around a hospital, but damn it, we know how to give virtual meds and start a Zoom conference!

These days, when I'm not staring at the ceiling, longing to program an IV pump, or pacing the sidewalk outside my apartment for the thousandth time, looking for unsuspecting pedestrians to practice my IV skills on, my new sheltering in place activities include reading the latest pandemic news (what did our president say today?!), stress eating everything out of my pantry, taking online quizzes to figure out what

Chipotle burrito I'm most like, and wait for it—completing my mandatory, somehow state-approved, virtual simulation! The very same clinical I was scheduled to attend this quarter at a level 1 trauma center in downtown Seattle. (It's fine. I'm fine. Everything's fine.)

Virtual nursing is basically the same as real life nursing except that literally everything is different. As a virtual nurse, I can assess, plan, treat, and even evaluate my own patients, but I can do so on a laptop, in the comfort of my very own home, with sporadic, almost musical stomps that I look forward to every day, coming from the 4-year-old tenant who lives above me. Life as a virtual nurse is going great.

On the bright side, I'm really good at converting pounds to kilograms and discerning what counts as a liquid and what doesn't. (Fun fact, Jell-O and pudding count as a liquid, but mashed potatoes do not.)

Luckily, I had completed the majority of my nursing education before the pandemic. My roommate, on the other hand, just started her first med-surg quarter, arguably the most difficult class, and has to learn the bulk of her nursing skills online. Try having a Zoom meeting where your instructor shows you how to prime, hang, and administer IV push medications to a patient who in reality is a coat hanger hooked onto a command strip. I never again will take for granted the many hours I spent in open lab, poking those silicone arms with dull needles and expired saline solution.

I am currently in my psychiatric rotation of school, which is of course online, and already, it's been noteworthy. There's something chilling about staring into the eyes of all 25 of my fellow classmates and no longer seeing the bright and eager nursing sparks that once resided, but in their place, a dull, soul-sucking black abyss, slowly draining any and all happiness with each minute of our three-hour lecture.

It was especially bad last week when our very intelligent and kind, yet slightly technologically challenged instructor accidentally clicked the speed icon during a "What's it like to have Schizophrenia" Ted Talk. You can already see where this is going. We all watched in disbelief as we listened to the speaker re-enact one of her schizophrenic episodes at double the speed, while our poor, flustered instructor was at a complete loss as to how it went so wrong. To her credit, we now have a new appreciation for, and can empathize with, those who suffer from schizophrenic tendencies, so that's something, right?

As frustrating as my experiences have been (and they really have), I am honored to be a nursing student in 2020. I am incredibly proud of those nurses who are currently kicking ass on the front lines of COVID-19, working until their legs give out, with bruised and cut faces from the protective gear they have used multiple shifts in a row, and who are verbally and physically assaulted by protestors who somehow think they are the problem.

I am forever indebted to the compassion, love, and sacrifice nurses have for their patients, especially during this pandemic, and I cannot wait for the day I can give back and fight by their sides. This fresh-off-the-computer nursing student is eager to help those who are giving their all and will join them as soon as she possibly can.

To all the nurses of this pandemic, from the bottom of my heart, thank you, and I will see you soon.

PANDEMIC GOT YOUR JOB? NO WORRIES: QUARANTINE SKILLS TO BEEF UP YOUR RESUME

by Eloise O'Loane

Of all the scenarios my chronic low-grade anxiety panned out, I've got to say—a worldwide pandemic was not one of them. It is no question that the global impact of COVID-19 will ultimately change society (for better or worse? Only time will tell). Of the many worst-case-scenario articles I can't seem to stop reading, a few have hinted that we may see a potential 30% unemployment rate in the near future (for context, the unemployment rate during the Great Depression was a little below 25%).

So whether you're just about to "graduate" college after a Zoom video conference commencement ceremony and enter the work force or if you simply pride yourself on always being prepared, I have re-branded nine skills you may not have even realized you have picked up during quarantine:

Remote Communication Skills
(Calling Your Parents to Cry Every 15 Minutes)
Every time I check social media or the news and see another terrifying statistic, I immediately call my mom to ask when all of this will be over. Unfortunately (like many of us) she does not know the answer to that question and has started sending my calls straight to voicemail.

But—this could absolutely translate to an improvement on my remote communication skills as I now understand how to verbalize my thoughts in a collected manner (and that you can use your phone for things besides looking at memes).

An Ability to Maintain Concentration and Focus (Running Out of Shows to Watch on Netflix and Actually Doing Productive Work)

Have you ever been so bored that distractions have no influence on you and you actually start being productive? I don't think any of us found ourselves here pre-quarantine life and now look at us! Getting. Shit. DONE! And by "shit" I mean the bare-minimum. Now go pat yourself on the back because no one else is allowed to do it for you.

Autonomous Self Starter (Not Lying in Bed All Day)

You did it—you dragged your body from the bed, all the way to your kitchen, and then onto the couch. That is something to be proud of in these trying times and a skill that will surely impress your future employer.

Strong Interpersonal Skills (Talking to Yourself)

I genuinely enjoy my own company—I'm a delight. But after spending so much time with just myself?? I cannot stand this bitch! I've resorted to thinking my thoughts out loud as a way to make it feel like there's someone else in the room and I must say it has significantly reduced the tension between us. I cannot stress the importance of understanding one another's (or even all the voices in your head's) communication styles.

Solution Oriented Problem-Solving Skills (Using Alcohol as a Coping Mechanism)

I'm no chemist but I'm pretty sure alcohol is literally a solution and I've definitely been using it to forget my problems. In fact—many CEOs of large, successful companies have used this as a coping mechanism—so there has to be something to it. Now where'd I put my hard seltzer?

Content Creation Experience (Shamefully Downloading and Making Videos on TikTok)

In the world of marketing—content is king. And learning how to utilize the newest forms of social media is a very transferable skill. Just, like, probably don't show people all those saved drafts of you attempting to 'throw it back.'

Responsible Resource Management Abilities
(Only Using One Perforated Square of Toilet Paper at a Time in Fear of Running Out)

Since greedy-as-hell folks took all the toilet paper when I was actually running low and needed to replenish my stock, I now have to deal with the consequences and significantly monitor my usage. I also have to take the extra step of asking the cute check-out clerk if I can get a pack of toilet paper and now, he knows I actually use the bathroom (humiliating). But not for naught, as through the trauma I have learned the importance of rationing—so thank you.

Self-Discipline and Impulse Control
(Not Eating All of Your Quarantine Snacks in One Sitting)

This was definitely a quickly learned and necessary skill once they started making us line up outside of grocery stores. I've managed to stretch my Trader Joe's Dark Chocolate Peanut Butter supply from one to two whole weeks—and that's on #portioncontrol.

Critical Thinking Skills
(Managing Your Anxious Thoughts as They Play Out All the Possible Ways the Pandemic Will End the World)

Let's be real—"critical thinking" is just a fancy way of saying "over-thinking."

All jokes aside—this is a difficult time for everyone. Whether you choose to spend your time watching Tiger King on Netflix or learning new skills (i.e., knitting, speaking Italian, or for some of you nasties—washing your hands), don't forget to give yourself, your friends, co-workers and family a virtual pat on the back for making it through a global pandemic.

SELLING POT DURING COVID-19

by Jamie Colson

The COVID-19 crisis has shaken up the daily routine for everyone in this country. The cannabis industry is not only surviving this crisis, it's thriving. Cannabis seems to be recession proof. Those who are lucky enough to have the essentials with some sort of savings or unemployment to live off of are also increasing their cannabis consumption to help the anxiety, pain and the thought of a post-COVID-19 future.

While we are forced to stay in, and avoid anything that normally keeps us sane, why would we not spend our days ordering Grubhub, binging *Love is Blind* and smoking copious amounts of weed? Maybe not everyone is doing this, (I prefer *Love Island*) but judging by the increase of cannabis sales during COVID-19, people are bored, they are anxious and they need their organic CBD, as soon as possible.

I've worked in the cannabis industry since 2014, starting in the black market right before it turned into *420 Shades of Legal Grey*. Most days I am proud to say I sell weed to every Dick and Jane that would like to get high before they do some yard work, but the bigger picture shows we still have a long way to full decriminalization and legalization at the federal level, (not to mention the disproportionate people of color still locked up for cannabis charges). I feel grateful and guilty on a daily basis. This job has been an emotional rollercoaster with increased inclines and drops during COVID-19.

It's interesting working as a guinea pig in this emerging market. There is no official set of rules for customer service like there is in a Nordstrom's or Starbucks. Sometimes we make it up as we go, everyone is new at this. And now we also get the pleasure of learning how to "budtend" in a pandemic. I never expected to be selling drugs in gloves and a mask to people complaining about their kids being out of school for the rest of the year. Welcome to Oregon.

People are stressed, they are overworked, and sometimes have no idea what they are looking for. We get the request for "Stevia" instead of "Sativa." For the record, we don't sell sweeteners. Some days we have younger, more informed customers. They are only looking for Indica Hybrids, high in terpenes, mostly Myrcene, grown inside organically, trimmed well, not cured too long, cheap, smells like unicorn farts, is gluten free and has a fair-trade sticker.

Times are weird. We have to be kind. We have worked incredibly hard to make our work environmentally safe, comfortable and compliant so that new, nervous and regular customers alike feel at ease when they shop at our dispensary. Our lobby is welcoming, and we have two small separate rooms for shopping, each with the same products, one budtender, one cash register with room for one customer at a time. This flow of transactions sets the stage for people to open up with the Budtender. People are used to the old days when buying weed was a different world. It feels like the awkward hangout time with their dealer has lingered into the legal era. Only now, instead of sitting on a couch in a dank, dark basement, you're standing at a counter, asking about different jars of weed and going on and on about your loud neighbors who have nine people quarantining in their two-bedroom apartment.

Every customer is different, and we can't forget about the OG smokers! The ones who have been "smoking since before you were BORN little lady" (they always put the emphasis on the born part). They want skunk bud. They want Panama Red. They need high potency. Nothing gets them as high as that old school weed. They love to tell us all about it—paranoia, seeds, stems, and all.

Selling weed can be heavy. We briefly play the role of a bartender or therapist where customers have the need to tell us why they smoke to cope with this or why they smoke to forget that. People are compelled to share anything: treating their cancer, losing their child to an overdose, what tacos they had last week, anything about their pet's kidney stones, and even stories of serious war injuries. Now, they smoke to forget that they are forced to stay home with their families. They complain about anything related to COVID-19—they can't go to Costco unless they put a mask on, how fake and made up this whole thing is. Then, the rollercoaster changes route and the next customer explains they have MS, saying how much they appreciate us for taking it seriously, and how they feel safer because of our cleaning procedures.

People have been either impatient or grateful as we sanitize after each customer. Some people have masks and stay as far back as they possibly can while ordering. Others come in with no mask, and proceed to lean their entire body weight on the counter and complain that we won't let their roommate shop next to them. There is almost no in-between at this point; people are panicked or respectful or they blatantly don't care.

Cannabis isn't going anywhere. Legalization is only spreading and hopefully before we know it, no one will ever fear of being imprisoned for a gram of pot. I could spend hours writing about what is wrong with the industry, but there is always more good than bad. People can sleep better with a low-dose edible. People in chemo can get an appetite from a strong Indica they tried. People with anxiety can relax a little after some CBD. An elderly artist can paint again after using some cannabis lotion.

Right now, people are coping in any way they can, and if that means cannabis sales are going up, then hopefully our spirits are too.

Community

PANDEMIC PARTY

by Marie Steinwachs

Hurray! The stay-at-home restrictions have been lifted and many parts of the country are re-opening! It is the middle of the pandemic, but you have to appreciate U.S. optimism.

No doubt a million small celebrations are being planned for that short window of opportunity between now and when the expected second wave of disease could hit in about three weeks (or maybe this winter, depending on which wild-ass guess you subscribe to) and we are all quarantined again. These guidelines are offered to help ensure your party is fun and reduce the possibility that your guests all become infected and your party becomes a widely cited national superspreading event.

1. Guests

The CDC recommends no more than six people at a gathering, so it is more important than ever to think about your invitee list! You don't want huggers, smoochers or touchy-feely friends, and you certainly do not want to include people who habitually spit (i.e., most men). In fact, you do not want to invite anyone with known bad hygiene; not right now.

Since we are trying to grow from this pandemic experience, maybe it is a good time to invite people who might have been on the "B" or even "C" list of potential invitees in the past—like those with hand washing compulsion, zealous germaphobes, or those whose "personal space" has always extended beyond six feet. In all cases, you are better to stick with close friends who know how to keep their distance.

2. Venue

The venue for your party must be able to accommodate six chairs, arranged in a widely spaced circle, at least 6 feet apart. Look at the pandemic as a great opportunity to throw a garden party! If you have no garden, a lawn or parking lot will do. Be considerate that your festivities do not overlap into a neighbor's yard or a sidewalk, where your guests could be exposed to, or are more likely to congregate with other company-craving people.

In some areas, it may be tempting to use the near empty public streets for your party. Technically they are your streets to use, but it does put your guests at greater risk of being run over by an ambulance.

3. Weather

It doesn't pay to plan a party farther ahead than an extended forecast. It really is inconvenient that the virus is driving our gatherings outside at the same time that hundred-year weather events are forcing us to cram together inside. Before you send out invitations, check your area for approaching hurricanes, blizzards, and other major hazards. Rain could put a damper on your party, but too much sun can do just as bad! Hopefully you were able, during your stay-at-home, to track the sun's advance across the sky, or even build a backyard replica of Stonehenge. You would have noticed that the light moves across the yard at a slightly different time each day. If you hadn't noticed, trust me that areas that are shaded today may, at the time of the party, lie several feet into the scorching, late afternoon sun.

The easy solution is to prepare for all possibilities by mustering up six umbrellas (a.k.a. sunshades) or suggest guests bring their own. An umbrella contest, with prizes for the largest, smallest, most unusual, etc., is a fun activity and a great way to get people to bring their own without letting on that even if it starts to rain buckets they can't come into the house (see Activities for more ideas).

4. Attire

This may be a good time to retire the notion of fashion altogether and invite guests to wear what is comfortable. They will appreciate the chance to model their sweatsuits and muumuus in public for the first time. After months of home quarantine, don't assume your guests will think of it if you don't mention "unmentionables." If you are squeamish, you might suggest that undergarments are appropriate. The one required accessory that is wildly popular and totally indispensable is the face mask! Folks with sewing machines are claiming new status and often exaggerating skills, and nearly everyone can select from a variety of intentional and unintentional mask styles proudly displayed on social media.

It is totally up to you to decide if you want to set a sort of "dress code" for the face or if you are OK with one of your guests showing up wearing a coffee filter. I'm surprised someone hasn't come out with party-themed facemasks yet, but it is only a matter of time before masks are available for every holiday and occasion.

5. Food

It complicates any pandemic party to serve food when the simple act of not touching things other people have touched becomes nearly impossible. Forget about the unsanitary

practice of sitting around a big table to eat together, much less eating something another person has created, with their own hands. Instead, a buffet table could be set up with space for each person to bring their own food! To make it even more festive, check out the many YouTube craft classes for how to make cute name cards for each designated section.

You may need to assist your guests in navigating the new food queue etiquette, especially if alcohol is being consumed. Consider installing a narrow gate to herd them into a single-file line, large arrows towards pointing one-way movement, and two end-to-end yardsticks to demonstrate proper spacing. Hand sanitizer should be provided at the start of the food line, though it is important that handmade or "craft" sanitizer is clearly distinguished from salad dressing or other condiments. And now it is both socially acceptable and politically correct to use disposable plates, utensils and cups. Your guests will be too appreciative of your attention to their safety to judge you for your wanton waste of resources!

6. Activities

Because of what we have learned about virus transmission, it is very important that your party does not engage in activities that could result in heavy breathing, singing, long boring oratories…in other words, activities that often involve alcohol.

Charades is a wholesome, natural activity for the pandemic party because you will certainly struggle to hear each other when seated six feet apart. Also, in some demographics it is highly likely that at least one guest will lose a hearing aid when removing their face mask to eat. By incorporating Charades, frustration is turned to fun as guests act out the dialog ("first word, two syllables, rhymes with 'pyrus'"). Incidentally, this kind of conversation eliminates a great deal of idle chat.

Finally, be sure to allow some time just for attempted conversation. After weeks and months of diminished human contact, people naturally want news from their friends—like where to get good hand sanitizer and whole wheat flour.

I hope these common sense guidelines help reduce the anxiety of having a party during a pandemic, especially since you may already be stressed to the max just dealing with the threat of the disease, unemployment, political unrest and supply chain interruptions, and the irritating quirks of others you may be sheltering with. No, it might not be a good time in general but that does not mean it is not a good time to party. Looked at from another perspective, it might be the salvation of our sanity.

A NON-AGGRESSIVE VIDEO CHAT INVITATION

by Halle Zander

Hey Old Friend,

I know it's been about thirteen years since we last spoke, but I was hoping you might find time in your schedule to sit down for a cup of coffee with me and catch up over Goom, Headtime, Boggle Hangouts, or any platform you prefer. Are you still interning at Radio Shack? Do you still host that book club for recent college grads?

If you have some time, that would be great. Do you have roommates nowadays? Do you think they'd want to talk too? If your dog is a good listener, you could just set me on the ground with them as you go about your day. I've been told my energy is similar to that of a house pet.

I hope you're surviving during this strange time of quarantine. I've been spending a lot of quality time with the internet lately, re-watching all of the classic shows from our youth like *Boy Meets World* or *A Shot at Love with Tila Tequila* or whatever videos come up on YouTube when I just type in "girls kissing." Anyway, that Topanga was just a riot! And it's too bad Tila turned out to be a Nazi.

I want you to know that I'm still here for you during these trying times. If you are feeling down and need a shoulder to cry on, I can recommend some of the best online therapists. Most of them are studying to get their bachelor's degrees in psychology, so they typically rotate between a handful of clichés. But it gets the job done, and I use it as a tax write off because investing in myself is critical aid for my community.

If you're available in the next few days, I'd love to share with you some of the old music I'm revisiting. Did you know that SPORKify can guess what music you played on repeat during high school on your CD player while you sobbed quietly under the bed? They made me a playlist called, "Crying into the Shag Carpet," including Evanescence, Alanis Morissette, and Avril Lavigne. It really brought me back to some painful, repressed memories that I'm hoping to share with you openly and honestly. Does that sound like something you can handle?

I've been thinking back lately to all of the fun times we spent together, drinking absinthe on the quad and running away topless from the campus police shouting about anarchy and government drones. Do you remember when we hid in the cactus bushes and got sent to the emergency room? Or the time we got into a meth-induced rage and ripped apart our bunk beds? What crazy times! I think that was you, wasn't it? If not, don't mention any of that to anyone.

So I'm free from 6 - 11 p.m. Monday through Sunday to virtually meet up. If none of those times work for you, I'm sure I can move some things around to accommodate you. And if you want to follow me on Instacracker, my handle is @quarantinequeenareyouup. (This way, my privacy is very secure!)

Sincerely,
The Girl Who Sat Two Rows Behind You in Political Scientology

Second Email:

It looks like your email bounced back, so I guess you're asleep. I'll try to resend tomorrow.

THE JACKALS

by Lauren Klein

I would have gone insane if it weren't for the wild jackals who hang out in my backyard at night. Before we were friends, I used to listen to them with annoyance—they were always running up and down the back alleyways, chasing each other, snarling loudly, and knocking down the trash cans. Didn't they realize the local insomniacs might be trying to lie awake in peace? At a time when death was all around us, it sounded like the guardians of the afterlife were brawling in my backyard.

I've always been a lone wolf. In high school, I ate lunch in the library every day for three years so I could be alone. When I was in the 12th grade, the school banned students from being in the library during lunch. "So they banned *you*," a friend pointed out when I told him this recently. Going to the cafeteria was torture for me. I sat alone with a book and pretended I didn't mind. Relatives and teachers told me that when I got older, I'd "find my people."

But I've never run with a pack. Now, separated even from my few close friends, it was starting to feel like I was alone on an empty tundra. Lying awake one night, I realized that some of the books stacked on the floor by my bed were the same books that had kept me company as a kid. Suddenly, I didn't want to be a lone wolf anymore. With no end to this vast expanse of solitude in sight, I wept.

Time in quarantine passed like a never-ending, broken train—my life passing by me. For four nights, I couldn't sleep until dawn. On the fifth night, I played a sleep meditation guided by a man with a deep, ominous voice. He invited me down a dark corridor towards "the most relaxing door I could imagine." As I started to follow him, I could hear my eggs crying to be fertilized, like dogs whining to be walked. It was ovulation day. Touching myself didn't help; I'd been doing that all night.

While my guide was describing the doorknob at length, I composed a text: "You weren't very good the one time we had sex four months ago, and although you may have thought you made me cum, you didn't. But it's ovulation day and I really badly need a fuck. Are you interested in helping me out?"

But it wouldn't be right to break quarantine with a booty call, so I deleted the text. "Breathe in and feel the breath spreading to every corner of your body." I thought about the Virgin Mary and wondered if anyone would believe me if I emerged from quarantine five months pregnant and claimed immaculate conception. "Let this breath ease you into sleep." The gong rang. Was I asleep? Was I dead?

A crash came from the yard. I opened my eyes and peeped through the curtain. The jackals were playing some kind of game. I went out on the back steps to watch them frolic in the moonlight. Seemingly unconcerned with the state of the world around them, they were chasing each other around like in a game of tag, except "tagging" someone meant going for each others' throats. Before I turned away, I thought I saw one of them smile at me. Just a little. They looked skinny; I wondered how their city food supply was these days.

The next night, I got up as soon as I heard them and laid out an array of snacks on the kitchen counter: some sliced apples, moldy tofu from the back of the fridge, toasted pita with hummus, and a bag of chips. As usual, they were mucking around in the yard. I waved to them from the back steps and gestured to the open door.

A pause ensued, during which they all looked around as if considering their options. Then they charged the door as a pack. Pushing against each other as they all tried to squeeze in at once, the jackals brought a heady, musky stench into the kitchen. They devoured the snacks immediately. One of them seized the bag of chips and tore it open with its teeth until the seam burst and chips showered the kitchen. After getting the room's attention, another tossed a tomato in the air and swallowed it whole, then stopped with a look of horror. Silence fell. Scrambling, eyes bulging, it extracted the vine with its paw, and the rest of them burst into raucous applause. Another one opened the fridge and started toss-ing beers around. We toasted, followed by more applause and cheering.

Their liveliness was infectious. I watched them in fascination. It wasn't hard to pick up their language; they speak an earthy, yet refined dialect, with a highly intuitive slang. Sitting around in the kitchen, some on barstools, others on the countertops and stove, we schmoozed with complete abandon. I hadn't felt so light-hearted in months.

One of them suggested making chai masala and was met with great en-thusiasm. Once the tea was ready, they started to sing. They sang a strange melody, in scratchy voices, all in different keys. But I found it soothing and peaceful. In the window behind them, the blue light was starting to strengthen. I felt sleepy and started sinking. One of the jackals crooned, "time for slumber." I told them they could all stay as long as they wanted—they only had to shut the back door behind them when they left.

Now we hang out every night. Periodically, they leave offerings for me on the back step—squirrel skin, acorns, dried figs with bits of garbage stuck to the peels, and once, a large marijuana plant, clearly ripped out of someone's garden, judging by the clumps of dirt caked onto the roots. Scavenger gods indeed. I always accept the gifts graciously.

The more time we spend together, the more I get to know them. One by one, I've learned their names: Snarg, Pumpel, Lynux, Herod, Shrap-nel, Arsh, Flacck, and Steve. Hints of interpersonal drama surface from time to time, but for the most part their camaraderie is seamless.

Their sense of humor is different too. The first time I heard a joke was from Shrapnel, apparently the comedian of the group. We were all sitting around the kitchen counter, drinking tea and smoking joints. Lynux said, "Tell a joke, Shrapnel!" Bashful, Shrapnel shook his head. "Tell a joke! Tell a joke!" Lynux started the chanting and the others joined him. "Tell a joke! Tell a joke!" They got louder until Shrapnel burst out grinning and gave in.

Silence fell. "Okay, okay. What did King Solomon say to the Ace of Spades?"

"What? Tell us!"

"At least you're not a spatula!"

I still haven't grasped their sense of humor, but I appreciate their read-iness to laugh.

The biggest surprise was that they loved music. I was shocked when I turned on the stereo and saw them halt, prick up their ears, and start dancing in ecstasy. They're especially fond of soul funk, '70s R&B, and disco. Their dance parties are trancelike and exuberant. We forget time, forget the outside world, and dance with no self-consciousness until it's light out.

I don't know what's going to happen. Most likely, the rich will find a way to profit from this catastrophe while the rest of us are too busy trying to survive. A feeling of powerlessness keeps me up during the day. But for now, I'll drink chai masala prepared by jackals, listen to their stories, smoke with them, and dance until the sun begins to rise.

A DOG'S LIFE, OR IS IT MY LIFE?

by Adina Gillett

I took my dog to the vet a few weeks ago as she was having, ahem, digestive issues. After looking under the hood, the vet determined that she either ate something disagreeable like a mushroom or a tampon and it would pass, or she was stressed that we are now home all the time.

What? My beloved, doting, devoted dog is *stressed* that I'm home now? She should be doggie thrilled. Is this not the culmination of all her doggie dreams? Nay, sayeth the vet (adjusting his roguish velvet tunic)—as much as she loves you, the change in circumstances is scary for her. She knows something is wrong.

She's right, of course. There is something wrong.

No, not the fact that our President is an ambulatory pustule (although she's right about that)—it's that she knows the world is whacked right now. Dogs (and dare I say, most animals) are smarter than we are. They are finely attuned to the earth and emotions and smells and sounds that we don't notice because we're way too busy catatonically scrolling memes to notice. I've learned a lot from my dogs in these past few months of isolation.

The wildlife outside really is fascinating:
I used to watch my dogs vigorously patrolling for squirrels and rabbits from the living room window and think, "So simple! So easily distracted!" And now, I find myself at windows, scanning the greenery, hoping for any sort of creature to make an appearance. I hear the rumbling of vehicles in the distance and wonder with a melancholic smile

what kind of vehicle it might be. Is it a car? Who's in it? Do you think they are alone or with a passenger? If there's a passenger, do you think they are housemates so it's safe? Do you think they are wearing masks in the car, or not? Or maybe it's a delivery truck, bringing goods to some lucky person's home. I wonder what they ordered. A bulk package of Cheeto Puffs? Some off-brand yeast packets from China that may or may not be yeast but the mystifying urge to bake sourdough bread is strong enough to risk it? Perhaps it's a drill bit set with that one bit size that could only be found in this set, which is really a waste of money but it's always handy to have another drill bit set and how did it get to be 11:30 a.m. already? Okay, dogs, I get it now.

Sometimes sneaking up and shoving your nose in someone's crotch is exactly what they need in that moment:
It's so easy to slip into isolation even within my own house and family. I've noticed that we all, in our efforts to adapt, are establishing burrows in various corners of the house like moles in a field. Yes, we all share this field, but we have our own holes which we've demarcated with a boundary of urine just to be sure there's no misunderstanding. And I think that's important right now—to have a space that feels like your place to go reset or read or study or play games or shop for drill bits or ponder the Latin derivation of the word "bored."

Food is a really big deal:
Yes, food was always a big deal, survival-ly speaking, but this is different now. Eating is now an event that breaks up the day, and not just a mindless and necessary activity.

When my husband is preparing a meal, I watch him with a cozy blend of appreciation, wonder, adrenaline, anticipation, and excitement. Look at him go! Some of that is for me! Look at those opposable thumbs! Yes, I have those too, but they are comfortably at rest right now, which is nice. And then, I get to *eat* it! Probably seated and relaxed rather than mindlessly standing at the kitchen counter like I did before. Overall, a much more significant event that it was before. Okay, dogs, I get it now.

A bad haircut isn't that big a deal:
The groomers are closed. My dogs don't shed. Their hair just grows until their eyes are hidden behind furry curtains and they walk around the

house like giant chia pets. I girded my grit and took to the trimmers. The dogs now look choppy and stray, but they can see and, best of all, they fit through the dog door again. They don't care. I don't either. That's it.

Having my belly scratched feels amazing:

Okay, maybe not my belly, but *touch* in general.

Wow. That's the stuff. With the fear of death from outside contact like hugs from friends, haircuts, massages, random high-fives from strangers when I bust out a winning quip in the Starbucks line (it's happened twice, okay?), squeezing into crowded elevators, even being bumped by hurried pedestrians—it all adds up to being touch-deprived. I even miss getting punched and kicked in Krav Maga classes. Who knew I'd miss the bruises and pain? It's hard to even imagine being in that studio again, all up close in some other person's sweaty business trying to dislodge their sweaty hands from my sweaty neck. *Did we actually used to do that?!*

I'd come home from my full-contact day and my dogs would be going nuts wanting to be touched and I'd be like, "Whoa, settle down there, girls, needy much?" And now, I just get it. They didn't get any rogue high fives in the coffee line or massages or learn self-defense while I was out. They just patrolled for ne'er-do-well wildlife and napped, utterly touch-deprived. Okay, dogs, I get it now.

We still need to make new stories and adventures right now:

I think a key to mental survival in this time of isolation and overall bedlam is to keep feeling like we are progressing and growing in some way. The other day, I took my dogs out for a walk and one of them dove into a hedge. I heard much furor and turned to find her emerging from the hedge with a rabbit in her mouth.

Mortified, I shouted *"drop it"* with my best SWAT team commander voice, which she obligingly did. I raced over to find the poor bunny in an advanced state of being shaken, not stirred. My dog stood there and watched it quickly expire, and I wondered what she was thinking.

"Did I do that?" Or "Oops." Or maybe "I'm sorry, I reacted out of doggy instinct. I'm not entirely domesticated much as these humans are wont to think and I truly apologize for my actions, although I can't feel entirely guilty because I was bred for this and it would be silly to self-flagellate over something I truly had no control over." Hard to say.

These are the kinds of events that make up the stories of lives—events both good, bad, and confusing that give us pause and reason to contemplate, fodder for bar talk later when we are all allowed to see each other in person again. We still need to do things to feel alive, to honor our instincts and then grapple with the consequences. Not that I'm advocating rabbit slaughter (or any other kind for that matter), but there is something to be said for connecting to our wild and undomesticated selves. Yes, for those furry types among us that might be chasing rabbits, but for others it might look more like going for a run. Or learning to grow food. Or playing online trivia with friends. Or finding a new job. Or finally asking that person out. Or writing articles about dogs in quarantine. You know, theoretically.

Dogs are really not that different from us. We are all stressed right now, even if on the surface things might not be catastrophic. Then why am I having these digestive issues? Maybe I just ate a mushroom or a tampon. It happens.

ROCKIN' IN THE UN-FREE WORLD

by Bethany Grace Howe

Out on the road the other day, I found the traffic quite light (amazing what a pandemic of congested lungs can do for congested traffic). Within moments I was cruising nicely along, the wind blowing in my hair much like Sarah Conner's as she headed off in her Jeep for Judgement Day in *Terminator*.

As always when I drive, I had the tunes cranked up, my choice of music matching my mood: "It's the End Of The World As We Know It (And I Feel Fine)." And I did. I felt fine. After all, I had gotten toilet paper at Costco.

What I didn't have was another song to listen to. Much to my surprise, my music streaming service doesn't have an "Apocalypse Mix" playlist. Accordingly, I reached out to my brain trust while sitting at a stoplight: "Tell me," I wrote on Facebook, "your favorite song about the apocalypse. I can't think of anything besides R.E.M."

The response was immediate: "What are you, stupid?"

No comment.

To say there's a lot of songs about doom I was forgetting is an understatement. Flying along in my Toyota Corolla Wagon—I'm sure it was Sarah Conner's second car—I was quickly on a "Highway to Hell," sadly aware that everywhere but Fox News "Another One Bites the Dust." But happily, we're all "Stayin' Alive," by surgeon-style handwashing and social distancing, so "I Don't Fear the Reaper."

As I drove on, however, and the suggestions from my Facebook friends continued to roll in, I realized three things:

1. I probably hadn't gotten enough toilet paper.
2. In these terrible times, one thing remains clear: The world needs more of the cowbell.
3. My friends are all sick and twisted people.

Within another hour there were more than 50 other songs on my playlist, each one drearier than the next: "Standing At The End of The World," "The End," and "The Earth Died Screaming."

That most of my friends are women probably somewhat explains this list. In the testosterone-driven dystopia where Harvey Weinstein was allowed to freely roam the world until very recently, it stands to reason women would be quicker to pull the trigger on how to musically pull the trigger. It explains, for instance, why someone's suggestion of "Eve of Destruction" prompted another friend to quickly come up with "Christmas At Ground Zero." Of course, even in the post-apocalyptic world, women would probably be expected to buy and wrap gifts, and clean up the mess afterward.

Other feminine connections revealed themselves. First: when it comes to songs to drink alone to, no one can match Matchbox 20. "These Hard Times" and "Mad Season," for example. It shouldn't surprise anyone there's a woman behind the band's success. Her name is Mama Jan Smith, and I can't help but feel that she knew social distancing was building like dark clouds on the horizon. "Long Day," "So Sad So Lonely," and "If You're Gone," are just a few more of Matchbox 20's greatest hits. I also think as a mother, Mama Jan forecast being stuck in the house with one's kids: "Put Your Hands Up," seems about right for the times. My friends certainly think so. "Keep Your Hands to Yourself" came up more than once in their suggestions.

Indeed, within a matter of minutes it became very clear to me that the women in my life are capable of creating more than just an apocalyptic playlist. They got down to the heart of surviving COVID-19 itself: "Can't Touch This," "Don't Stand So Close to Me," and "I Can't Feel My Face." All of them now seem less like songs and more like life lessons from Dr. Phil, who even with his Texas twang and a gun probably still couldn't get through to those idiot kids partying in Florida.

From all of this, it might be tempting to think that all my female friends are twisted people – and they kind of are. We covered that.

What they also reminded me, however, is "I Will Survive" and we are all "Headed for the Future." (I never said I wouldn't write a tortured mess of a sentence.) They reminded me that Matchbox 20 has this covered, too: "Back to Good."

For even in the hardest of times, it's women who time and time again move us forward, getting us past today's troubles. And none more so than my friend's mom, a hard-scrabble, Texas-bred woman in her 70s, who's survived a lot, but who's compromised immune system has kept her trapped in her home for weeks. A woman who despite these barriers to happiness had advice that was simple, and yet profound: "Why Don't We Get Drunk and Screw?"

Nope, can't touch that.

THE HILL

by Chika Ekemezie

When quarantine first started, I barely knew how to ride a bike. I learned late in my adolescence (age 11) when after several tearful summers, punctuated by me accidentally tearing up my dad's legs and being dumbfounded at the concept of balancing on a bike, I rolled down my driveway and smacked into our mailbox.

But as the weather got better in the spring and cases began to drastically decrease in Washington, DC, my bike and I developed an intimate relationship. It began when I realized that the brakes were totally shot, and she needed some love from a bike shop. And love I gave her. I fixed her brakes and got her some new front and back lights. I even got a cute little rearview mirror that I affixed to her handlebar.

For the first three months of quarantine, I basically lived in the suburbs. When small groups began to gather outside, there was no way for me to meet my friends in a park. I had to bike nearly 2.5 miles so we could meet each other halfway.

My roommate and I decided that this wasn't sustainable, so we decided to move closer to the heart of the city. This new apartment was *everything*. We had a fancy brick wall that was the perfect backdrop for non-stop Zoom calls. We lived walking distance away from the Metro—not that I was comfortable using it during a pandemic—and we lived much closer to the under-30 crowd. Our old neighborhood was located right by one the best elementary schools in the country, which is fine, but it doesn't make for the most exciting place to live for a 20-something.

Anyway, moving our new apartment brought me much closer to a group of friends of mine. Rather than having to bike 40 minutes to hang out on their porch, all I had to do was pedal for a mere 10 to 15 minutes and I was there. Except for one thing.

The hill.

They say Washington, DC is bikeable, and for the most part, I agree. But the hills are ridiculous. Early in my biking career, I made the mistake of cruising down a hill for a good 10 minutes, not realizing that I would have to find a way to get back up there (I walked).

The hill on the way to my friend's house is one of the worst hills I've experienced. It was steep for a few hundred feet, which is bad on its own, but just when you feel like your legs have completely turned into cement, there's one more intense incline for you to navigate. In that moment, it's as if you're suspended in zero gravity, barely moving. It feels like reality has stopped and nothing exists except for you and the hill. Until a douchebag honks at you for moving too slowly (we're supposed to share the road, asshole!).

So, I'm left with a decision. My friends on the other side of the hill have space. A porch. A large backyard with a *badminton net*. All the (relatively) safe COVID-19 activities that a girl could ask for. There's only one thing stopping me from all those activities. That goddamn hill.

Every time I'm on that hill, I begin to wonder to myself. "Maybe being alone for weeks on end while your roommate is in Connecticut is fine". "Maybe you don't need human contact to function". "Maybe crying yourself to sleep because you're lonely is better than going up this fucking hill."

But it's not. I need to see my little COVID-19 pod. And so, like clockwork, one to three times a week, I hustle my ass over that hill, decrying gravity and God every single time.

COVID-19 has wrought a lot of havoc. But in 2021, when you see me with thighs of steel, you'll know why.

The hill.

Relationships and Sex

HOW TO KEEP YOUR MARRIAGE ALIVE (IN THE TIME OF COVID)

by Laura Wheatman Hill

So you're stuck at home with your spouse during self-isolation. This is not a time to let your marriage die. Think of this as an opportunity for reconnection, both spiritually and physically. No need to social distance from your significant other.

Follow these 10 tips for a fun, sexy quarantine:

1. **Assure that you're healthy.** You don't have coronavirus, do you? Wash your hands. Take a shower separately. Then together. It's too late now, anyway. Die together, like Romeo and Juliet, but with more wheezing.
2. **Board games.** Make sure they don't have too many rules. Your mental health cannot take complicated, multi-step games. You can play Pandemic…but should you? You're already living it. A better idea would be to add sparks to your relationship by making every game the strip version: Strip Scrabble, Strip Hungry Hungry Hippos, Strip Pandemic. You get the idea.
3. **Shave. Or don't.** You can embrace your cavemen-like, raw, primal instincts along with your caveman-like pubic areas. Bodies are sexiest in their natural state. I'm sure there's some research about that somewhere.

4. **Watch something together. Nothing sexier than the *Tiger King*.** Scary movies always put you in the mood for a snuggle? How about that Netflix pandemic show? Or…? Or take your mind off your troubles by finally watching *The Wire*. You know you (don't) want to…

5. **No clean clothes? No problem.** Let it all hang out. You're not hosting anyone. But, on behalf of your neighbors, do close your blinds.

6. **Cook together.** Sure, the meal might be a slapdash assortment of canned beans at this point. Why not make a chili with garbanzo beans? Get creative. Throw in some butter beans. The couple that farts together, stays together.

7. **Keep the mystery.** Save power. Turn off the lights. You're broke AF now that you're unemployed and you could use the electric savings.

8. **Compliment each other.** Like this: "Honey, I appreciate how you've been rationing your toilet paper." "Why thank you, dear, and your thick eyebrows are coming in quite nicely." Even when you feel annoyed, try to see the good in each other: "Darling, you load the dishwasher so creatively." "How sweet of you to notice! Yes, and you make the most delightful chewing noises first thing in the morning."

9. **Let it Go.** Do you have kids? Good. Because, if you do, you'll be watching *Frozen 2* at least once a day. Even non-parents can take a tip from the ice queen, "Let it go." There are big problems, like the economy's collapse and a potentially deadly disease that you may or may not have been exposed to, and there are little problems like "What are we going to do today now that we have no jobs or anywhere to go?" and "What is that smell? Is it me? Is it you? Is it the dog?" Either way, during this time, let it go. Relax. Enjoy your time together.

AND OUR LAST TIP:

10. **You can't afford a divorce right now.** Maybe you get health insurance through his work. Maybe she's the only one with an income now. Either way, you certainly can't be moving into separate apartments at this time. You can't have a day in court. Court's not in session, you guys. So, make it work. Because it's really your only option right now. Time to break out the Strip Qwirkle.

THE QUICK AND DIRTY GUIDE TO DATING APPS: GLOBAL PANDEMIC EDITION

by Hayley Zablotsky

In college, my friends called me a serial dater. This means that I went on a lot of dates with a lot of interesting and ultimately disappointing people—people who squelched my hopes of living a Regency-era romance novel, my desire to eat at Olive Garden ever again, and in some cases my very soul.

It was inevitable that I ended up on the dating apps, which led me to write this Quick and Dirty Guide about navigating what can be a truly shocking, albeit occasionally wonderful experience (especially for newcomers). Now here we are, in the midst of a global pandemic, and dating app usage has spiked off the charts. So, I've updated this dating app guide for people like me who are still trying to find love even now as the world seems to be ending.

I. The Basics: First, let's talk about why you're here on this dating app. What are you looking for? Casual sex that may or may not give you syphilis? A wedding date? A pen pal? A Netflix password? There is no wrong answer. You might think these apps are just for hookups, but in reality, people use them to find serious relationships and other random things like weed suppliers. It's a brave new world out there.

First, let's talk about why you're here on this dating app. What are you looking for? Casual sex that may or may not give you syphilis? A wedding date? A pen pal? A Netflix password? There is no wrong an-swer. You might think these apps are just for hookups, but in reality, people use them to find serious relationships and other random things like weed suppliers. It's a brave new world out there.

PANDEMIC UPDATE: Unfortunately, it is no longer a brave new world. Kissing is literally illegal. Using these apps will only lead to ex-treme sexual frustration, longing, sadness, and possibly an *almost-but-not-quite* partner—perhaps a lovely, genuine person with blue eyes and a killer recipe for eggplant parm. Perhaps you'll really like them, and per-haps you'll want to date them exclusively and more seriously. But how are you supposed to bring this up in the current circumstances? How can you want to date someone seriously when you've only met them in person *once* before the world went into lockdown? What would it even *mean* to date someone seriously right now?

Here's what it seems to mean: looking nice (but only from the waist up) for video chats and taking online quizzes together that answer press-ing questions like, "What Kind of Potato Would You Be?" When your date gets the results that they'd be a "plain old russet potato," you can reassure them endlessly that, to you, they are a fine and fancy potato (this is the serious commitment/real relationship part).

II. Your Profile: Your dating app profile is crucial for your success. You need to have at least four photos. Your first photo should be of just you. There is nothing more frustrating than squinting at a bunch of photos of the same fifteen frat bros, trying to figure out which one is Spencer. Spoiler: He's not the one you hope he is.

Your second photo must include an animal, preferably a dog. This says a lot about your character. And if we know *anything* about online dating, it's that character matters above all else. Your third photo should in-clude a few friends to prove that you're cool and that you have friends (provided you have friends). Your fourth photo should be of you doing an activity that shows how fun you are—a corn maze, perhaps, or a boat ride with you wearing a bulky orange life jacket.

Your bio should be pithy and welcoming. Don't just say you like tacos. Everyone likes tacos. Also, don't say you love "going on adventures" be-cause no one knows what the hell that means. It could mean a perilous journey across the high seas in search of lost treasures or it could mean a drunken 2 a.m. trip to the Steak and Shake. Personally, I'm only up for one of those (the second one). Be specific.

PANDEMIC UPDATE: Going on adventures of any kind is now illegal. Also, if you no longer look like your profile photos (i.e. you haven't worn pants since February, you have a unibrow, your hair is growing out in a strange new color, etc.), don't worry about it. You have bigger things to focus on right now like 1) teaching your grandparents to use Facetime, 2) attending to your rapidly declining mental health, 3) coming up with new ways to cook with pasta and canned beans, and 4) showing off your pasta and canned bean recipes to your grandparents on Facetime.

III. Their Profile: If a bio says, "I'm hardly ever on this app, haha," assume that they are *constantly* on the app, including right now while they're on the toilet. If a bio says, "God is First" and/or "I am Second," double-check to see if *your* bio also says this. It's good to be on the same page about Jesus. If you're not, your date might tell you that you're going to hell (it happens).

If the *first* photo of someone's profile is of a cat, proceed with caution. Similarly, if you come across a bio that only has photos of damp pieces of paper that say "I am more than my appearance" written in Sharpie, don't engage. Watch out for Chad.

PANDEMIC UPDATE: If you find someone you're interested in— perhaps a lovely, genuine person with blue eyes and a killer recipe for green chile enchiladas—don't bother. You probably won't get to see them in person until you're both grandparents, except that you never *will* be a grandparent because that would require having children, which would require having sex, which doesn't seem to be something that will ever be an option for you again.

IV. Opening Lines: The first message—whether you send it or receive it—is everything. Does it have grammatical errors? Don't ever go out with someone who confuses "your" and "you're" because who knows what other horrors hide beneath the surface. Does it have the word "fuck" in it more than twice? Is it a pickup line? Pickup lines can be fun but should be unique. Anything involving fallen angels or phone numbers is dumb and unoriginal. Try something fresh like this instead: "Are you an appendix? 'Cuz I don't know what you do but I'd love to take you out." Or maybe don't say that. It's sort of gross.

PANDEMIC UPDATE: Here is an example of an inappropriate but fast-spreading pickup line: "If coronavirus doesn't take you out, can I?" Say no. Alternatively, if they ask you about your *Star Wars* opinions, always engage and promptly pledge to them your life, love, and fealty. Then, decide to dress up for Halloween together in a *Star Wars* couple's costume. Then, realize that you're planning to still be together at Halloween. Realize the effort this will take. Realize that you're both committed, even though you've never even watched a movie together—only simultaneously, which isn't the same thing. Realize that someday you will watch *Star Wars* together. In the same room. On the same sofa.

V. Other Tips: Dating apps may end up bringing a lot of stress into your life. Make sure you rant to your friends about "the system" or societal norms or the economy or your parents' divorce or whatever else you feel like blaming this mess on. Alternatively, dating apps might bring you much-needed human connection. Unless, of course, you're not talking to a human. Don't ever provide your credit card number. Or the three numbers on the back.

PANDEMIC UPDATE: Above all else, whatever you do, do *not* fall for somebody on a dating app during a global pandemic. Not even a lovely, genuine person with blue eyes and a killer recipe for green chile enchiladas. But you will, despite this sound advice. Dating them over Facetime will feel strange but also really right at the same time. And you'll want to hug them, just hug them, more than anything. And they'll want to hug you too. They'll tell you this through a computer screen, while they sit in a house just across town and a million miles away. It'll be terrible and bizarre, but it will also give you tremendous hope about the resiliency of the human spirit and the transcendent power of genuine connection. You'll wonder if this relationship is viable, if there's any point, but you'll ultimately decide yes, yes as long as you want to hug them. And you do. You'll want to hug them more and more every day it remains against the rules. You'll never take hugging for granted ever again.

Anyway, don't say you weren't warned.

PORN IN LOCKDOWN: AN ITALIAN WOMAN'S (NOT-SO) GUILTY PLEASURE

by Laura Magnani

When Christian Grey pronounced, "I don't make love. I fuck. HARD," he was not facing a quarantine alone in a tiny apartment in Italy.

Given that we are all trying to cope with the resources available to us, we can safely say that, even when it comes to sex, we have rolled up our sleeves and taken care of things without making too much of a fuss.

If on the one hand COVID-19 has limited our life, on the other Karma met us halfway. In this case, Karma has a name: Pornhub. If you're unaware, Pornhub is one of the most clicked, free pornographic sites in the world.

Starting on March 12th, 2020, the day after the announcement of the national quarantine in Italy, it offered a "premium" section free of charge to all Italians. That same day, visits to Pornhub increased by 57%. I think that Italians, with every single click, are paying the mortgages on the super luxury homes of the website's owners.

And part of that 57% increase? Women.

That's right, we women watch porn. We masturbate. We even masturbate while watching porn (it's called multi-tasking, duh!).

For women in 2020, porn is no longer a taboo. In Italy, for example, 29% of users on Pornhub are female. And the number has increased in the past decade.

The main difference between men and women when it comes to pornography, lies in the choice of porn we choose to watch.

The numbers have increased so dramatically that the "female-friendly" category, dedicated to the female audience, has been replaced by "popular with women." We're not looking for friendly; we're looking to get off.

I know that most people like to think of masturbators as possessing a penis and a giant box of tissue (which is in short supply), but the porn industry has finally started to understand that not only do women want porn, but we want something different than what titillates male customers. And also that we can say the world "titillates" without giggling— most of the time.

When it comes to porn, as with everything else, we women have more complicated tastes—I would search something along the lines of, *"well-endowed man that turns me upside down as I would with my home when I can't find the car keys,"* for instance. If in the past women used to watch a porn video for purely "educational" purposes, such as finding new ideas and inspiration to seduce or boost a relationship with a partner, now the aim more often than not is purely sexual pleasure.

In a porn video, a woman wants to see a representation of herself, according to an article I recently read on *The Cut*. And she does that by looking for those elements that can represent her real passions. Passions such as yoga, for instance. Apparently in 2015, for example, A yoga-themed orgy video drove a massive spike in yoga-themed searches on Pornhub. The appeal, it seems, is the wardrobe: yoga pants, ripped yoga pants, and tight yoga pants were all more popular than naked yoga.

In Italy, yoga is really popular but not to the point of becoming a sexual fantasy niche. I mean, when I practiced (I admit I'm a bad student), I didn't experience any particular increase in sex drive when I tried the tree pose or the bridge or the corpse. Rather, I felt mostly pain and shakiness.

Italians are people closely tied to tradition. We much prefer the sexy mechanic character or the plumber that saves the day with a plunger rather than a yoga pose. At best, we would like some porn variations in theme with our quarantine experience. How about Amazon courier porn? It would be an awesome quarantine plot: Closed stores. Online order. Amazon courier. Mask, gloves, condom, sanitizing gel before and after, me dressed as a package at the front door, crazy sex while I'm being unpacked, and then off he goes for another delivery. Or maybe, for the bold, a storyline with a threesome at our Prime Minister's house. Perhaps, porn with remote-controlled vibrators, just to be practical during social distancing.

These days, looking for a porn video on the internet is easier than going to the supermarket—you can skip the lines and forget the facemask (unless you're into that). You just log on, choose the product, and consume it. It's that simple. And no one wants the same thing day after day; one day you may want chocolate croissants and the day after, a sandwich with corned beef and sauerkraut.

Nobody can see you. Nobody can judge you. Online porn can make you feel sexually free in a way sex with a partner IRL may not.

What is certain is that we Italians have deeply missed physical contact, in whatever form it could be experienced.

WE DON'T GET TO PICK OUR QUARANTINE (S)HEROES

by Joanna Collins

My pussy has never rioted, but it has held a silent protest; and, most recently, it has been on government lockdown.

Picture this: the year was 2020, and it was February. Now, the exact month is quite critical to this story. I had just wrapped a run of *The Vagina Monologues* in Nashville after nearly a year of rehearsing, preparing, and howling at the full moon with my fellow *Vagina Warrior* sisters. Performing this seminal feminist play with a community of incredible, liberated women—in front of a thundering live audience —left me feeling electric and empowered. Strap on a hard hat (and maybe a strap-on) because I was about to shatter every glass ceiling in sight. I was riding a riptide of feminism and busting at the seams with both sexual freedom and a desire to uplift other women. I've always been more of a Venus Flytrap than a wilting flower, and *The Vagina Monologues* gave me the confidence to be even louder in my demands for equality and independence in all areas of life. I even had my eyes on a clitoral stimulation vibrator that looked like an insect and had wings that nestle around your labia. WINGS! Flapping around for my pleasure! I am woman; hear me roar with self-generated ecstasy!

So, of course, at this exact moment, the universe sniffed out my extreme confidence and ordered me to put my vagina away. The pandemic arrived in full swing in March, just one month after our final curtain call, ushering in a thousand uncertainties. As the door slammed shut on my panic room, I had nothing but time to scream questions into the abyss: Would

I have to storm the gates of a Charmin factory to procure toilet paper? Should I order a bidet? Why was everyone hoarding condiments? And, most importantly, would my dear Venus Fly Trap ever eat in public again?

I feared that my vagina would become a vestigial limb if I didn't use it soon. I didn't want it to be simply symbolic, a badge of honor, a shuttered nightclub filled with dusty disco balls, telling the story of a life once lived. No, I wanted it to have the second act that it deserved. Acknowledging that "use it or lose it" is not actually how evolution works, the situation felt dramatic and dire, nonetheless. Plus, focusing on the complete non-issue of my sudden compelled abstinence felt better than falling to pieces about the actual horrors around me. I could keep perspective. I could also root around the couch cushions for my lost vibrator and make it work. Nevertheless, she persisted, right?

But then, just when I started to think that I could be my own quarantine hero, my worst fears unfolded before me. On top of the global pandemic, I faced a series of unfortunate personal inconveniences (note: unfortunate, not tragic). They were the type of quandaries that make you exclaim, "Oh brother! Here we go again!" Essentially, my own home started to turn against me like a haunted Queen Anne cottage in a horror film.

It started with a busted toilet (who knew a toilet could just...break?), but, pretty soon, my car and other major household appliances wanted in on the fun. It was like that episode of *Small Wonder* in which Vicki (the child robot) gets electrocuted, and all the household electronics start demonically turning off and on. Again, my worst day was like a 1980s family sitcom so, all things considered, I was pretty lucky.

Disclaimer notwithstanding, imagine living in a one-bedroom, one-bathroom condo and suddenly finding yourself with a possessed toilet. I will spare you the details but believe me when I tell you that I tried my best to troubleshoot and, regrettably, failed miserably. The hours I spent watching YouTube videos on toilet repair were all for naught. That's what I get for double majoring in "Theatrical Faces" and "The History of First Ladies" in college.

It became shockingly apparent that my strong suit was not basic life skills and home repair. I'm handy, but not like that. As a single attorney in my thirties, I feel compelled to show the world that I could make it on my own. This was especially true in the wake of *The Vagina Monologues*; I felt like I was letting my sisterhood down with my ineptness.

Which is why it pained me so much that, at every turn, I had to have a man bail me out. I rationally knew that *The Vagina Monologues* is not about men, and it's certainly not a takedown of them. They are an essential part of the story, but it's not about villainizing them or removing them from the equation. We didn't say, "boo, men!" even once! It is a call to action for everyone to join the cause and topple the structures that damage us all.

Some of my best friends are men.

Despite this, I was dripping in girl power and in no mood to have to be saved. But, like most inconveniences, my home repairs were indifferent to my desires. The universe might as well have tied me to the train tracks because I was officially a damsel in distress. I needed men. Men to unclog a broken toilet; men to replace said toilet; neighborhood men to jumpstart my car; professional men to replace my car battery after the jumpstart failed; men to return power to the grid in my neighborhood. CAUTION: MEN AT WORK, SAVING ME.

Plenty of qualified women work in these fields, but god thought it was hilarious to send me a series of men to save the day. I had been working on my Michelle Obama arms in quarantine (read: lifting 1-pound Zumba weights) so that I could slay my own dragons! I felt small and deeply unnerved at the reminder that, no matter how hard I try, some things will always be out of my control. I wanted to clean up my own messes, but I was coming up short.

However, just when I started to spiral into pandemic panic, a fellow *Vagina Warrior* texted me simply to check on my well-being. We talked poetry and toilets, and she offered me the use of her bathroom if I needed it. A true queen shares her throne. I knew that she was managing a thousand stressors, too, not least of which was mothering in the middle of a goddamn national emergency. Yet, she made the time to send me a burst of love and support. She didn't minimize my problems or tell me that it could be worse (even though it definitely could); she was simply there for me as a friend.

In that moment, I realized what a chucklehead I had been. *The Vagina Monologues* weren't about doing it all by yourself. They're about lifting up the voices of women in the community.

Women don't have to be jacks of all trades (plumbers, auto mechanics, contracts lawyers, Zumba enthusiasts) in order to deserve respect and independence. We don't have to prove our worth; we are already worthy. It was okay for me to acknowledge my limitations and call a professional (especially because my home remedies of mixtures and potions had actually clogged the toilet further). It was okay to ask for help.

Invigorated, I tore the couch apart to see if I could find my long-lost vibrator. My vagina deserved a treat after all she'd been through this week (Month? Year? How long have we been in quarantine?). There were so, so many crumbs between the cushions. But, also, a quarantine miracle! The prodigal son (or daughter!) had returned. And I was about to save myself. At least for the next ten minutes.

A DIGITAL DATING DOOZY AND OTHER ONLINE DISASTERS

by Carmen Woodruff

Nine months into quarantine. A bulging belly but no baby. I'm feeling bloated, yet festive, just in time for the virtual holiday dinner shuffle: the dosey doe where I bob and weave my way through inquiring minds who demand my current dating status. I've gone from a "How to Lose a Guy in 10 Days" case to a "How to Lose a Guy in 10 Minutes" success story. Thank you, God, for Zoom mute capabilities and camera *off* options, not to mention "that shoddy WiFi service" conveniently seeping into the conversation when certain topics arise.

In addition to my COVID19-pound weight gain, I haven't been to the threading place in ages. My eyebrows have reached new horizons in all directions. Thank goodness for the facemask now required to cover areas that otherwise—pre-pandemic—would've showcased my smooth and supple welcoming signature smile. *It's all I had left.* In the good ol' days back in February, I may have had a shot at attracting the man of my dreams. But today, as I make my 11th weekly and unnecessary *get-out-of-the-house* Target drive-up run, I courageously venture into the store with the hopes I'll casually air bump into an eligible bachelor. We'll high five elbows and the rest will be history.

Woosh! The cold Midwest air slaps me in the face on the way out of the store and back into reality, my arms filled with new nighttime snacks. *Girlfriend, you are nowhere near attracting the man of your dreams.*

Maybe the man of your screams! My mind wanders as I've consumed far too many Investigation Discovery episodes. I return home to safety where my DVR is filled with *Real Housewives* drama and the latest *Bachelorette* show. I channel my inner Tayshia Adams, following her journey in sunny Palm Springs where I coincidentally spent two weeks in the same exact resort for job training. If I close my eyes, I'm almost there! And then I try on my bathing suit in nostalgic glee. Wrong move!

Switching gears, I whip out my cell to see who's new on the five dating apps that have been on my phone since Donald Trump won the election in 2016. I reminisce about my summer social distance date with—let's call him "Tim". After a promising interaction on Bumble, we met via video around July or August of pandemic 2020. He seemed pretty normal: a fellow musician with a lot of heart and ambition. We thought it would be fun to have a podcast-esque adventure. He'd play for me his favorite songs and I'd do the same.

2.75 hours into the date, I blast "I Can Change" by John Legend as we near our 3-hour stopping point. I'm bobbing my head to the beat as I introduce the song as a pretty darn near close description of the kind of guy I'm looking for: a straightedge gentleman who stands up for his woman. I'm lost in the comforting lyrics of the song and spoken word combo of the two male narrators—John Legend and Snoop Dogg. They've seen the light when it comes to treating a woman the right way. And I see it too...

"I won't get high if you want it...I'll get right if you want it. Go to church, get baptized if you want it…"

I sing along.

Out of my peripheral, I spot Tim rolling up a piece of brown paper about the length, width and circumference of my two index fingers if I position them together. Think Chinese finger traps. He's stuffing it with something mossy in color and texture, circling back around with his thumb and right index finger, using his mouth to seal his creation. We lock eyes and he sheepishly says, "Is this a dealbreaker?" I try to form an open-minded sentiment but mumble something probably indistinguishable. Out of politeness, I blurt, "Next time we'll..." and I can't even remember what I said. Deep down in my debutante, "Ain't I a Woman," such-a-lady-but-still-a-feminist heart of hearts, I was *appalled.*

And that was my last contact with a man during this pleasant quarantine journey.

In a last ditch effort after ample recovery—I guess—I returned back onto the apps. This time, I went old school, apprehensively opening my MacBook Pro lid to join Match via my mom's final recommendation (aka threat). What the hay! I'll give it one more shot. Funny thing is, as this particular dating platform grows archaic compared to its competitors, it kind of mirrors me as I reach slower ticks and tocks of young adult days. At least it will be filled with respectable men who know how to treat a gem.

Scrolling. Scrolling. Scrolling.

I add the mobile app to my phone for instant notifications in efforts not to miss Prince Charming. Ping! *You have a new like...It's Tim.*

I'm done. The app shop is closed for now as is my search for a suitor in the year of quarantine. My trips to Target will continue and I'll pair them with a focused fitness plan, a mirror and a journal to re-introduce myself to the me I've always been: a lady of valor and value with or without a man on her arm.

RELATIONSHIP ADVICE FOR SHELTERING IN PLACE

by Lori Barrett

Shop for the lockdown and come home with, among other groceries, four cans of soup. Learn this is an alarming lack of soup.

Be too particular about toilet paper. Until it's too late.

Join the dog in staring out the window. Mention how deserted the street is.

When he responds, say, "Wait, hold on. I just thought of the perfect song for my quarantine playlist."

Ask Alexa to play "Breathing" by Kate Bush.

When your daughter is forced to come home from college, retrieve the individually wrapped take-out forks you'd insisted she take for use in her dorm and place them in a pile in the dining room because they might be useful at work.

Continue going to work as a sort-of essential person at an essential business. Never bring the forks to work, so when your husband walks past them every day, he can mutter out the first syllable of your name.

When he coughs, yell from the other room: "Did you cover your mouth?"

Ask where Joe Biden has been.

As you're eating lunch, describe what you saw a woman doing with her chewing gum, with her hands, before she reached out to touch you. Too descriptive.

Ask if asparagus soup sounds good for dinner.

Instead of thanking him for vacuuming, tell him he forgot to turn off all the lights he'd turned on while vacuuming.

While he's actually working from home, take a break from Twitter to offer unsolicited advice on how he might do his job better.

Ask where Biden has been. Again.

At dinner, as your husband clears the plates, say you want to save the leftovers. They'd make a good lunch if you put an egg on top.

Look out the window; see a group of young men, one in mime makeup. Call into the other room to ask your husband what they might be doing.

Accidentally store the quarantine-size bag of onions next to a heating vent.

Open the window to mitigate onion smell, until he can't work because the apartment's too cold.

Suggest watching the new season of *Vanderpump Rules* together.

Watch *Succession* instead, but spend the entire time messaging a cousin and asking what just happened on YOUR show.

With the toilet paper situation critical, stop him on his way into the bathroom and ask him to rate the urgency on a scale of 1 to 10.

Suggest saving leftovers again. To eat the next day with an egg on top. Smile serenely as he gestures at the refrigerator and says: "Stuff goes in here but it never comes out."

As a midnight snack, while awake and trying to figure out where Jimmy Kimmel got that amazing dining room sofa, eat the leftovers with an egg on top.

When he proposes watching *Succession* the next night, say you can't because you're shopping online for a dining room sofa.

Watch *Contagion*, about an animal-borne virus that started in Asia and becomes a pandemic. Find it oddly soothing.

Was Gwyneth Paltrow robbed of an Academy Award for that death scene?

Read before going to sleep, under a lamp as bright as the sun because you deemed lampshades at the stores a poor match for your bedroom, before every store closed.

Continue reading as he switches that lamp for the one from your daughter's dorm room.

Continue reading as he realizes that's even worse.

Stay awake thinking about *Contagion*, especially the violence that follows food shortages. Berate yourself for your lack of canned soup.

As he's falling asleep, ask if it might be a good idea to buy plywood to cover the windows.

Mental Health and Wellness

A CORONAVIRUS YOGA PRACTICE

by Wendy BooydeGraaff

Hello and welcome to Yoga in the Time of Coronavirus. We've had to make a few accommodations during this time of self-quarantine, and while we are not refunding any memberships at this time (in fact, we ask for your generous donations! Help us stay in business!), we invite you to join us to practice in the safety of your own home (or wherever sheltering-in-place is for you) with a few simple modifications. Themed yoga. The theme: Stay home!

We believe you will receive the full benefits of our yoga professionals by staying in your home while we inundate you with emails, vlog posts, and tips on how to stay calm while the flags are flying half-mast and you can't visit your aging grandmother or your newborn nephew. We've arranged a nice flow in these dozen poses, but as always, find what feels good, keep your hips square, and open your heart to the ceiling. And breathe!

1. Instead of Sun Salutation, try a *Neighbor Salutation* through the front window. Lift both arms up, inhale, and wave side to side. Exhale. Repeat. Also, it does wonders for the collective morale to practice elaborately safe greetings.
2. *Virus Warrior II*, with a disinfecting wipe on forward-facing hand and hard surface within reach. Pivot. Reach for the doorknobs! Remember: graceful, easy movements—it's all about flow—and multitasking yoga for pandemic times.

3. Warrior III is now *Fend Off the Kids Who Are Home from School with a Gentle Push from Extended Arms and Leg.* Add in a torso twist for the persistent kids who don't understand social distancing is for family, too. Inhale deeply in this six feet of space you have carved out for yourself.

4. *Lion's Pandemic Breath* is a good way to get that oxygen deep inside while utilizing PPE. Inhale through the nose, imagining the air around you is clear and virus-free, and exhale through your facial mask, or the front of your t-shirt, or if wearing a yoga bra, use splayed fingers. Work with what you have—wherever you are in your Coronavirus Yoga journey is okay, because it's *your* journey.

5. Tree pose. Similar to the classic pose, to remind you of what it felt like to go outside. Close your eyes, imagine the sun shining on your leaves, people picnicking below your limbs—balance, both for the body and the soul—this is essential, especially during these times. Commit to your breath. Inhale, exhale.

6. Boat pose, or more aptly, Floating Cruise Ship, Unable to Dock. Deep breaths. If you are shaking, send your breath to the place where your fear and tension reside. Breath into the fear. Exhale through the tremors. Deep breathing will alleviate any somatic sea sickness.

7. Yoga in the park—nixed for the summer—I know, it's hard, we could all use a little field trip outside. But, instead of Yoga *en plein air*, try this variation of Gate pose called *Close the Gate and Keep Everyone Out.* It's just like the regular Gate pose, but as you reach over, instead of opening up the side body, be sure to close the Gate and latch it. This can be literal or metaphorical. Don't let anyone in, not the delivery people, not your neighbor, no one!

8. Instead of Downward Dog, try the extended in *Quarantine Puppy*—add in a twist to chase your tail and be sure to knock over all glasses of water and cups of coffee! Your kids—if you have them—are still around watching (where else would they be?!), so invite them (or whomever you live with) to don some blue latex gloves and pet your back—it's going to be a long time before you can get a real massage. Breathe.

9. Next, move into the *Superstore Lunge* to get ready for that big outing coming up known as Shopping for Essentials. Lunge for the last hand sanitizer on the shelves. Low Lunge for the pack of wipes that dropped out of that man's hands when he was bumped with your cart. Low Lunge on the other side when you see your boss shopping midday and you are supposed to be "working" from home.

10. Supine Big Toe hold is now *Supine Big COVID-19 Toe hold*. This is the time to reach forward, grab the strap (or actual toe if you don't have a strap), and inspect your big toe. If signs of purple toes, lesions, or chilblains, drop strap, call your telehealth provider, and get tested! Then, check out our series on Yoga for COVID-19 sufferers, *Yoga on a Ventilator*, and *Yoga for Coronavirus Recovery*.
11. Child's pose remains a fairly similar comforting mainstay with a nice addendum. Stay here for several breath cycles, then turn to one side curled in the fetal position for an indefinite amount of time—perhaps for as long as it takes for the curve to flatten and/or TP is back on shelves.
12. Once finally asleep, wake yourself back up, wiggle toes, wiggle fingers, apply hand sanitizer to each finger in a gentle circular motion. Take this time for a gentle and hygienic self-massage. Breathe through the negative thoughts. No, TP may not be back on the shelves yet, but your yoga practice is expanding. You, combined with our Yoga in the Time of Coronavirus essential tips, are your own best teacher.

In closing, put your hands to your heart, then your third eye. The light in me honors the light in you—even in these virtual times. Release your thoughts to the air—the stale inside air you've been breathing for many months. Take this time of self-quarantine to practice yoga throughout the day, taking opportunities to interlace your fingers and shake your own hand, or wrap your arms around your shoulders to give yourself a hug because you're the only one who can!

I WON'T DRINK TO THAT

by Melody Dodd

Lockdown as a sober person is almost as nutty as being drunk. Every day the news is stranger and stranger. We've got gibberish coming from the White House. We've got people who object to wearing the very masks that might just save their own lives. When the mask vs. death debate emerges, the answer is so obvious, I keep thinking "I must be drunk."

There's never a wrong reason to get sober, but a global pandemic sounds like a decent one to me. It's weird that this medical apocalypse has put me in a state of gratitude I haven't felt since the early days of my sobriety. Should I feel guilty?

I can only imagine the additional levels of fear felt by those who must rely on alcohol to cope. They not only have to worry about running out of toilet paper like the rest of us, but also depleting their booze stash. So far, I haven't encountered a masked Saint Bernard with a mini-keg on their collar and a Solo cup balanced on their head.

By the time I got sober 28 years ago, I definitely had my drink of choice which was "More," followed closely by, "Are You Gonna Finish That?" Whatever was on special was a close third, and I didn't need a global pandemic as motivation to get tanked. So, I understand those who take to social media posting about their day drinking. Desperate times call for desperate measures.

It may also be the case that the "president" makes more sense if you're tanked—maybe double-speak at a third-grade level is only understandable to someone who is heavily intoxicated. After having watched several episodes of *Drunk History*, I do know that many of their loopiest guests make more sense than the man supposedly in charge of this country and fighting this pandemic.

And drinking to make reality make more sense is not an experiment I want to take on. I figure my date with the death is decades away and there's no reason to invite the Grim Reaper to the party any earlier.

Technology is a savior in this pandemic. Social media reminds me daily that there are like-minded people in the world. Recovery gatherings have moved to tablets and smartphones. They're a little different – it's tough getting used to making my own coffee. I've also recently discovered that a smartphone actually works as a telephone! Since the lockdown I've had many heartfelt conversations with beloved friends.

Some things that have helped me during quarantine: I've been able to perform in three live cyber-comedy shows and Zoom-meet with the improv troupe I'm a member of twice a week. There's nothing like shared laughter and creativity in community to reduce the sense of isolation.

I believe that's part of what I was seeking in the bottle—joy and connection. But to fully experience something, whether it's a friend's company or "dating" Hugh Jackman in your imagination, a clear head is required. That's especially true if one hopes to remember the event. I *love* being sober.

It's possible to do *all* of life's experiences sober—celebrations, holidays, and travel. Even more importantly, it's also possible to survive the tedium of daily life and the sad events of loss and grief without drinking

I must admit that I do have one big regret about my sobriety. If I'd only started saving the money I was spending on alcohol when I quit in July 1991, I'd be writing this essay from a lockdown in a far more exotic locale—say New Zealand, Jakarta, or Timbuktu.

But even with this setting, I make sobriety work for me.

EXTROVERT LOSES MIND
HOURS INTO SOCIAL DISTANCING

by Kate R. Canter

Local woman Serena Blair has fallen into violent mania after less than a day of staying home and avoiding crowds due to fears of COVID-19.

According to friends and family, Blair, 23, was initially excited to stay home from work as a Hollister employee.

"She decided the global pandemic would be a great opportunity to 'center herself,' get back into meditation and yoga," said sister-in-law Allison Blair, a first-grade teacher who will be out of work until April.

However, roughly six seconds into meditation, Blair was confronted with the inherent unknowable emptiness of existence. Within an hour of staring into the abyss, the Blair reportedly blinked just once.

The former Hollister employee and communications major documented her plummet to insanity on her social media accounts.

Like many Americans, she had stocked up on various essentials for the oncoming quarantine. An Instagram post, tagged as #prepper and #quarancation, displayed her inordinate supplies for a shared two-bedroom apartment. This post contrasted sharply with another, uploaded 45 minutes later, in which Blair had wrapped herself in toilet paper and proclaimed herself a living god. Then, in a tone believed to be influenced by marijuana, Blair whispered, "No one can know! No one can ever know!" before sending the video to her 5700 followers.

Another video, posted on Tik-Tok roughly two hours later, showed

Blair sinking slowly into a bathtub of Purell while repeatedly murmuring "this is fine" in a British accent.

Though she continues to avoid large social gatherings according to the CDC recommendation, Blair is not entirely isolated. Her roommate of two years, Lisa Ortiz, is also staying home from work and unnecessary outings. "I've had my headphones on most of the day," the 24-year-old Ortiz reported. "I have heard her pacing in the hallway during pauses in my podcasts. I really hope she doesn't damage the wall by rubbing her shoulder against it so much. She's asked me to come out and play a few times, but I'm actually getting tons of reading done."

Ortiz was ambivalent about her roommate's change in behavior. "Selena's usually at a party or her boyfriend's house. I couldn't say what she usually does, besides pass out on the couch." Ortiz then noted that she found the apartment on Craigslist and returned to drawing her webcomic.

Serena Blair's unraveling has also inconvenienced her building's supervisor, Francine Block, who had to screen her calls due to continued complaints by Blair of a small Victorian ghost. "Veronica won't let me sleep," Blair whispered in her latest message, "Veronica says Lisa brought the sickness with her. Veronica says the chimney boy has taken my jewels."

"This building was constructed in 1985," Block reported, "and Serena said she [Veronica] died in 1849. There's also no chimney in that unit, so I'm 90 percent certain Veronica is fake, but I'm not about to mess with some consumptive dead girl with everything else going on."

Appearing on her fire escape, disheveled in a long, white dress with several black and red stains, Blair declined to comment on her dwindling sanity. However, speaking through Blair's mouth, Veronica expressed excitement about the idea of a "cleansing fire."

FIVE WAYS TO STAY A BAD-ASS BITCH IN A CORONAVIRUS WORLD

by Christie Withanie

One vital part of being a bad-ass bitch is boldly wearing the attitude that you're not affected by anyone or anything. How do you let that persona shine when you're dressed like you're scrubbing in for surgery and you smell more like disinfectant than perfume? Keep reading for a list of 5 tips and tricks for remaining your bad-ass self while the Coronavirus has the world in a panic.

1) Remember that you are your own person.
No one can tell you what to do. You don't have to listen to the CDC when they tell you to wash your hands with soap and water for at least twenty seconds every time you pass a sink. No, when you wash your hands, you choose to do it of your own free will. In fact, you were doing that way before anyone was all up in your business, and you've got the chapped knuckles to prove it.

2) Talk to anyone that you want.
So what if you have a cold? So what if your bestie has a fever and the chills? No virus can keep the two of you apart because the internet exists! You can spend all the time you want with anyone you want using free programs like Skype, Google Hangouts, or an AOL bulletin board—complete with wine and all the tea you can handle. Additional benefits of this method

include saving gas money and the opportunity to avoid putting on pants.

3) You don't need a secret handshake.

Hugs are so yesterday. Even fist-bumping takes more energy and enthusiasm than most bad-asses care to exert. The environment is finally ripe for keeping your hands to yourself and not feeling bad for anyone if they sneer at you for leaving them hanging—and I'm not knocking elbows with anyone either.

4) Clear the cooties.

Have you ever felt like wiping off a surface while glaring at the last slob who used it? Go for it! You're not just satisfying your inner bitch, you're silently broadcasting a public service message. Those years of refusing to touch dirty bathroom handles are about to come in handy. Luckily, germ-wipes fit easily into most handbags.

5) Avoid sharing.

Tell Karen to get her own damn dessert and keep Kevin away from your drink. Splitting a plate is deflating, and it's also not very bad-ass. Now, you can keep your edamame, appetizer platter, and sake milkshake to yourself and enjoy every minute of it, thanks to COVID-19.

Let everyone else look at this pandemic as a time of terror and solitude, this is your time to shine. And, if for any reason you decide to self-quarantine, remember that bad-ass bitches need fuzzy jammies, too.

FOUR SIGNS QUARANTINE HAS GOTTEN TO YOU

by Mia DeSantis

If you are anything like me, quarantine has been kind of a blur. What day is it? Tuesday? Second Tuesday? Everyone has different ways of coping, but if any of these examples relate to you, quarantine may have gotten the best of you.

1. You Jewish Mother...Nature.

Throughout my quarantine journey, one of the skills I picked up has been gardening. I ordered a mini-jungle off the internet and now half of my room is dedicated to plants. In a past life, gardening gave me a tremendous amount of anxiety because I was in constant fear that all the plants were dying (why are they dying?!). To conquer my gardening anxiety, I am now mothering these plants. I am constantly making sure that they get a lot of sun, offering to cook them something every couple hours, and making sure that everyone is looking their best and getting along.

There is also a mother bird who set up shop in a pine tree next to my window and I am so worried about her! I am frequently checking on her, making sure that no asshole teenagers mess with her nest, and to tell her that she looks great even with the pregnancy weight. I also wish I could build her a little bird condo for when it gets cold and rainy. I have become a Jewish mother—always around and always offering snacks.

2. The Insecurities Get More Insecure.

Just because I can't go out does not mean I shouldn't still look good! Like many, I try to keep some sort of a beauty routine. I don't know if I have been spending too much time in my mind prison, but my insecurities go from zero to sixty really quick. It becomes the thing that I focus on for the entire day. Mirror, mirror on the wall...is one of my boobs way bigger than the other? I know having one slightly bigger is normal, but that looks A LOT bigger. I now need to try on all my shirts to see if it is noticeable. Just like that, my entire afternoon is gone!

It also magnifies insecurities that I didn't even know I had! Like my voice—is that how I've always sounded? Oh god, I sound like someone with laryngitis. Wait, do I have laryngitis? How did I get laryngitis? I have been walking around my entire life with this voice and no one said anything to me! That is worse than neglecting to tell me that I have spinach stuck in my teeth! THE BETRAYAL!

3. Writing Correspondence Like I am in The Civil War Era.

My Dearest Friend,

I do not know when last I heard from you, but it feels like an eternity. I, myself, have lost hope because I have finished my stash of Stan's Donuts and am unable to acquire more. Being deprived of their friendship reminds me of how I long to be reunited with you. Please send a word with haste so I know you are alive.
Your Best Friend,
Me

Being isolated from the world makes any interaction with another human being a precious thing. Due to the uncertainty of when I will be able to hug my friends or get to see their faces (and the plethora of dog videos I need to show them!), I make a boilerplate statement along the lines of "until our paths cross again, you beautiful unicorn." If you re-read your text messages and sound like Scarlett O'Hara – hang in there!

4. Time is an Illusion.
What IS time, really? In a household where everyone is working from home, I am just floating around looking for ways to pass the time. Most of my time is spent watching Netflix and hoarding snacks in my bedroom. I can neither confirm nor deny that I have growled at my parents to protect my snacks.

I keep attempting to have a plan for when life goes back to normal and the thing that trips me up the most is going back to the idea of "weekend plans. Not having the timeline of a regulated workweek erases the concept of the weekend—weekends don't matter anymore! NOTHING MATTERS. Silver lining though, I can no longer be late to things because I have nothing to go to.

That's how I'm doing in quarantine! In case you were wondering, yes this is what a mental breakdown looks like on paper. If none of these relate to you, congratulations! You can use this article to feel better about yourself. If any of these DO relate to you, fear not, you beautiful unicorn. We are all in this together and if you are lucky, you too can have snacks and a mental breakdown!

QUARANTINE DREAM INTERPRETATION

by Regina Velázquez

Looking for a Bathroom

Dream: You're desperate for a bathroom but can't find one. When you finally do, it's in an open space with no stalls. There isn't a square of toilet paper in sight. It's as if TP never existed.

Meaning: In waking life, you seek privacy. You can't have a Zoom meeting without some random person walking behind you in a bathrobe.

Action: Wake up 15 minutes early to lock yourself in the bathroom. Notice that when you close your eyes, everyone disappears. Be sure you have toilet paper or something
that functions as such.

Falling

Dream: You're falling through the air and can't stop. You see poles and limbs you could grab, but you're afraid to touch them because you dropped your hand sanitizer.

Meaning: You have a major problem in your life that needs to be addressed; you will feel no sense of control until the issue is solved.

Action: Do nothing. The only real problem you have right now is a pandemic. Enjoy the feeling of falling, which would cost you a hefty admission fee at Six Flags, but
you won't be doing that this summer. Make your own hand sanitizer from vodka.

Being Chased

Dream: You're being chased—slowly—by unmasked zombie-like grocery shoppers encroaching on your six-foot safe zone. They are not following the store's directional arrows.

Meaning: The people chasing you represent your inner demons.

Action: Consider the fears that might be plaguing you, such as your fear of getting sick, losing your job, or giving in to rampant alcoholism. Carry extra masks with you and hand them out to strangers. Employ your shopping cart as a social distancing tool. Use a lacrosse stick to scoop your groceries off the shelves.

Being Nude in Public

Dream: In the middle of a public place, you suddenly realize you're wearing nothing but a mask. One small, thin, papery mask. You may or may not be wearing the mask on
your face.

Meaning: You have been hiding a part of yourself from those around you, and you fear exposure.

Action: Stop oversharing your emotions on social media. Eat sensible meals at the table, as if someone were watching you, not fistfuls of Lucky Charms while slumped on the couch. Change your underwear, for heaven's sake. Order more if you have to.

Running Late

Dream: You were supposed to be somewhere at a certain time, but you're late. You can't find your car keys; you can't even remember how to drive. Public transportation
has stopped running. You're on foot, and you're trying to sprint, but all those quarantine cookies are taking their toll. You can barely breathe.

Meaning: You have taken on too many responsibilities in your life and are feeling stressed.

Action: No one is having this dream right now. Go back to sleep.

Seeing a Celebrity

Dream: You're sitting in your apartment planning what socks you'll wear today when suddenly in walks a celebrity. You are wowed, yet somehow this is all very
comfortable, as if a character from that show you've been binge-watching has stepped out of the screen into your living room.

Meaning: The celebrity represents a part of yourself that you would like to receive recognition for.

Action: Be sure you are truly asleep when you have this dream. Turn off all devices. You may be hallucinating. Go to the mirror and remind yourself that the celebrity does
not live in your house. Call your mother or any person who will be enthusiastically receptive to your call. Brush your hair if you're FaceTiming. You are always someone's star.

Catching a Cheating Partner

Dream: You discover your partner cheating on you. The other person looks as if nary a Cheeto has graced their lips in their whole life, and they've honestly been doing
ab workouts in their living room since February. The jealous rage you

feel is eclipsed by the terror of knowing your partner is bringing a fresh crop of germs into your bedroom.

Meaning: You feel that your partner isn't paying as much attention to you as you'd like. Perhaps the person is distracted.

Action: Take a break from reading the news, talking about the news, and asking your partner about the news. You are the one who's distracted, and it isn't helping your
relationship. Have you witnessed your partner going out anywhere? Has the front door been opened in weeks? Dig deep to find the issues inside yourself that are causing you to distrust your partner. Try something new to get your partner's attention: have a candlelit dinner, read a romantic novel aloud to each other, or dress up in a clown suit.

Taking a Test

Dream: You show up to an exam but have no idea what the class was about. You scroll and scroll through the Google Classroom notes, but all the comments are simply "When is this due?" and "Are we meeting Thursday?" The link to the exam seems to have disappeared. The teacher's office hours aren't for another week.

Meaning: You're feeling insecure about yourself and doubting the quality of your work, especially compared to the accomplishments of others.

Action: Allow yourself to be less than perfect during quarantine. Your ugly sourdough bread tastes delicious. Call two good friends and describe the true state of your kitchen floor. Let your kids have unlimited screen time for the day. Letting go of perfection means you're giving yourself an opportunity to go to the bathroom by yourself so you can stop having dream #1.

Flying

Dream: You're flying, floating, or soaring high above the ground, and your maskless face is breathing in the thin, clear air.

Meaning: You desire freedom from the quarantine situation.

Action: Keep dreaming, bub.

Losing Control of a Car

Dream: You're in a car. At first it's not moving; it's just sitting in the driveway. You're not supposed to leave your home, remember? Then the emergency brake slips, and the car begins to roll. You can't turn the wheel or brake. You crash in a horrific manner. An ambulance arrives to take you to the hospital. It, too, careens out of control, hurling and slamming you against the sides of the ambulance, but you somehow make it to the hospital. Attendants in full protective gear run out to wheel your stretcher into the hospital. Without warning they disappear, and your stretcher races down the long white hallway, threatening to slam you into a wall at any second. You can't stop the constant, destructive motion.

Meaning: Some aspect of your life is out of control. You feel that your destiny is entirely out of your hands.

Action:...nothing to be done.

FIVE WAYS TO USE MALE EGO AGAINST YOUR ABUSER DURING LOCKDOWN

by Giugi Carminati

Quarantine deprives us of more than just the ability to leave the house—it also deprives all of us access to "other spaces" and everyday autonomy. While others are mad about their roots showing and not being able to get a new tattoo, women locked down with their abusers have real problems. As things for all of us get worse, they get much worse for others.

While other helpful columns will tell you to call law enforcement, go to a shelter, or obtain a protection order (which in some places, like Colorado, can protect the home address and remove the offending party from home), I have some ideas for ridding yourself of a domestic abuser that are so far outside the box, you'll probably have to wash your hands after reading them just like you do after Instacart delivers your groceries. My basic concept is this: turn your abuser into a COVID-19 denier! Genius, right?

The reasons for doing this are simple: COVID-19 deniers are 1) less likely to tell you not to leave the house; 2) more likely to leave the house themselves; and 3) they may actually get sick (Consider their time in hospital your mini-vacation.) Look, I'm not wishing COVID-19 on anyone because it's bad form—but if a domestic abuser gets it (and doesn't spread it) am I really going to be sad about it? Uh, no. I've got 99 problems and feeling sorry for abusers ain't one of them.

Here then, are five ways to turn your abuser into a COVID-19 denier:

1. Sow the idea that COVID-19 is "not as bad as the flu."

Facebook memes and right-wing news pundits comparing COVID-19 to the flu do wonders for distorting data and spreading misinformation, so why not use this to your advantage? Turn your computer to strategically selected Fox *News* shows whenever your abuser is in the room.

Casually mention that a friend of a friend of someone you know said they had COVID-19 and it was "just like the flu" and they got better after "a few days or something." Be vague on the details but be adamant about unsupported and unvalidated scientific data. If you have to, refer to "a study you read" and "some research you did." Even better, find friends of your abuser and refer to their posts or statements. Look, do scientists and the CDC agree about the severity of the flu? Yes. But that guy you went to high school with, who still thinks antibiotics work on viruses, doesn't, so who is to say what the truth is? Embrace ignorance and use it to suit your purpose.

2. Discover an affinity for quoting "the President."

Between his daily misinformation word salad sessions and his toilet tweeting, you can find "the greatest, genius" quotes to support you in your quest of creating a COVID-denier at home. Just like this virus, Trump's misinformation and stupidity is everywhere. Take these two quotes, for example:

March 9th tweet: "So last year 37,000 Americans died from the common Flu. It averages between 27,000 and 70,000 per year. Nothing is shut down, life & the economy go on. At this moment there are 546 confirmed cases of Coronavirus, with 22 deaths. Think about that!"

Trump after meeting with Republican senators on March 10th: "It will go away. Just stay calm. It will go away."

If your abuser does not trust pussy-grabbers who call women "dogs who bleed from their whatevers" then this technique is probably not going to be effective. Move on to the next approaches and hopefully you will find something to work on your particular brand of abuser.

3. Explain that wearing a mask in public is "living in fear."

This country rapidly entered the Idiocracy phase of the COVID-19 pandemic, where lots of science-denying folk are yelling that "WEARING A MASK MEANS YOU'RE LIVING IN FEAR."

Make fun of people who wear masks and repeat the fact that masks are part of a government conspiracy to make us afraid to go outside. Quote an anti-vaxxing, flat-earth-believing government official who supports the idea that mask wearing makes you less of a man. This no-mask approach is a trickier tactic assuming you are still going out and about (and you're smart enough to always wear a mask in public). If your abuser sees you wearing a mask, it will undercut your efforts, so keep your mask in your purse or take up wearing scarves like Dr. Birx.

If you get caught with a mask, chalk it up to peer pressure or going to stores that require it so you're only wearing it "because you have to."

4. Make lockdown a feminist issue – if you need him out of the house.

Obviously, feminists have always had it out for men (duh!) but you can really lean into that with the pandemic. What does the COVID-19 pandemic do? Force people to stay home. Who is that hurting? Hard-working Americans (make sure to use "Americans" in there to underscore the patriotic aspect of this). Who are these hard-working Americans? Men! (Women are home taking care of kids, obviously, because that's what's "best for them."). So obviously, COVID-19 is a feminist conspiracy to take men's jobs away from them. The best way to fight back is for men to go back into the workforce, as soon as possible, like right now. (Not all men, just the one you're dealing with, but let's not quibble here).

5. Make COVID-19 an economic issue (which it is) – if you need to get out of the house.

If you need to get out of the house and into work (or just out of the house), then jump on the bandwagon that the economy needs to reopen right this minute, regardless of the human cost. Make it about capitalism, the right to work, the right to get a haircut so you can look attractive to him, the right to buy his favorite beer or whatever else pushes the right buttons.

Does your abuser hate it when others try to tell him what to do? Well, the government is definitely telling him what to do and telling you what to do, and only he gets to do that. (Look, we're leaning into insanity here, just go with me).

There you go! Five tips you probably haven't thought of. And certainly, all those pesky domestic abuse experts and non-profits don't have these suggestions on their websites.

UNHEALTHY WAYS I'M DEALING WITH THIS CRISIS

by Daphne Dot

As a single woman in London that lives inadequate paycheck to inadequate paycheck, I know a thing or two about stress. Questions that come into my mind on a daily basis are: do I have enough wine in the fridge? Is the man I matched with on Hinge plotting to murder me? And (a daily question) do I buy this expensive croissant to even out the never-ending joylessness of work?

I'm stressed, I'm skint, and I'm exhausted. Like, really fucking exhausted. And now, while I'm locked at home with bad WiFi and a mountain of work to do for my shitty job, I have to deal with self-described experts telling me how I should be coping.

Ah, yes, I forgot that middle-aged white men love nothing more than pushing their cocaine-laced noses into the collected private lives of women all over the country. Fantastic. I have heard the word 'unprecedented' more times in the past month than I have in my entire 27 years of existence. *It's not even that good a word.* A better word for the current circumstance? Shituation. Though that's not exactly in the BBC's brand guidelines.

Now, as well as being tired from work, wired from a day of staring at a screen, and doing around 131 steps daily, I'm annoyed. I'm exhausted, and I'm annoyed. I don't want people to tell me to watch out for my drinking in a pandemic. I don't want them lecturing me about my daily exercise when I have never been able to work out without a class instructor yelling at me in front of a larger-than-life and hugely unflattering mirror. I don't want to break my professional and personal boundaries and talk about my feelings with my boomer boss. I don't want to enforce no-screen time when the only thing that's currently bringing me joy is bingeing *Gilmore Girls* for the third time. Stop with the email marketing. Stop with the pointed displays of *faux*-empathy. Stop with the fucking video calls. *I am done.*

My life is not to be lived by best-practice guidelines. Give me the messy, unfiltered, barely-coping-but-fuck-am-I-trying-my-best views of life. Give me glorious, unhealthy coping mechanisms, like...

...BOOZE. Currently, I have two bottles of white in the fridge, a red and a white in the cupboard, a liter bottle of gin and two large bottles of tonic - and I'm actually not sure that's enough.

...ONLINE SHOPPING. I can't even tally up how much useless shit I've bought online recently. It's amazing how having all this extra time and few things to do except use a computer means you gravitate towards Oliver Bonas every 45 minutes. Those who say money can't buy happiness have clearly never fantasized about having your shit together and buying stuff under the pretense of making that happen. Yes, I do need that gingham dungaree dress. Yes, I do need that grey pom pom blanket to drape over the sofa to hide the mayonnaise stains. Yes, I do need a new set of dinner plates to upgrade the ones my parents bought me in IKEA when I was 18.

...SNACKS. Fuck, I love this one. My natural reaction to stress is to sweat and to snack. I've always had a sweet tooth - but when I'm under pressure this sweet tooth starts vibrating at a frequency only detectable by jelly babies. All that's running through my head is: "If I have to deal with this bullshit today I need at least three KitKat Chunkies." Stock up. Like, now.

...WANKING. Now this is a weird one because personally I have not felt sexy—at ALL—since lockdown started. There's nothing to quell your confidence like becoming one of millions of boring people doing n o t h i n g all day. You gain weight. You shower less. You stop wearing makeup. Your hair is constantly in a messy bun. It isn't the typical sexy look. When my FWB hits me up these days, I ignore him; I don't want to take pictures of my naked body when I feel my limbs are filled with peanut butter. But wanking? Different ballgame. I don't care how long it takes, I will watch porn until I come. I deserve orgasms. If I'm going to be lying horizontally the majority of the time, I may as well make it enjoyable.

...TAKEOUT. Now that I'm not spending hundreds of pounds a month on my commute, I can afford a weekly Deliveroo. I was never one to indulge before lockdown - but now I do it once a week at least under the guise of "supporting local businesses." (This is fantastic for those who start on the wine bang at 5:30 p.m. and forget to make dinner, which I definitely haven't done four times since March.)

...BATCH COOKING. So far I have made curry five times. Each time it makes five servings. My entire freezer is full of curry and one lonely box of fish fingers. All of my tupperware is going to be stained from the turmeric—but hey, *it's PC, right?*

...MIDDAY NAPS. My boss thinks I'm nose-deep in a project, but every day between 1-2 p.m., I'm asleep. It's delicious.

So to my single women, my partnered women, my lonely women, my happy women, I say to you—our call to arms—*fuck unmessy.* We are in a pandemic. *A literal pandemic.* There are no rules because who the fuck writes self-care survival guides for living through a—at the risk of re-peating myself—*fucking pandemic.* I urge you to put yourself first. Light your own candle, take care of your own needs, run your own scented bath and sit and cry and chug a G&T. But most of all: Don't you dare make yourself feel bad for it. We're all crawling to the finish line in the dark. See you there.

MY WEIRD QUARANTINE DIARY

by Stacey Gustafson

If you're like me, you've been holed in your castle, crib or dungeon, for what feels like a year. By the time the shelter-in-place announcement was made, I had already organized my canned goods from small to large, watched twelve videos on how to cut my own hair and learned how to whistle with two fingers. Now what?

With my newfound time, I started a daily quarantine diary to remind me of the weird, quirky, and funny things that have happened along the way. How did wearing a mask at the bank turn good and not wearing a mask bad? And now we handle an Amazon package like Tom Cruise disarming a bomb in *Mission Impossible?* I've been warning people for years that the sign of peace at church was the kiss of death. No one listened.

Here's what I noted:

Day 1 – Our grandparents were called to war. We're being called to sit on our couch. Together we can do this.

Day 2 – The dog refuses to eat dry kibble and I feed him chicken and rice, which he gobbles down. Due to shortage of chicken I'm faced with a new dilemma. If the dog starts eating chicken, then are we going to have to consider eating the dog?

Day 3 – Didn't realize the husband used speakerphone for 12 hours a day. Must seek a noise cancelling headset.

Day 4 – Grocery stores are out of milk. I guess we'll have to drink wine.

Day 5 – Stashed a few extra rolls of toilet paper under my side of the bed. One never knows.

Day 6 – Remember when you said, "When will I ever use math?"

Day 7 – Every disaster movie starts with the government ignoring a scientist.

Day 8 – If you wear a plastic dog cone, can you still touch your face?

Day 9 – Can I wear this mask to the bank?

Day 10 – Am I in love with Dr. Anthony Fauci?

Day 11 – Watching *Tiger King* for the first time. This is the stupidest show I've ever seen. What's with the mullet haircut? Wait one minute. Why isn't this guy on American Idol?

Day 12 – Loving the banter between New York governor, Andrew Cuomo, and his brother, CNN anchor Chris Cuomo.

Day 13 – Wonder who's really behind COVID-19, Charmin, Zoom, or Purell?

Day 14 – I can't do this.

Day 15 – I traded a friend a stick of butter for hand sanitizer.

Day 16 – My dog is giving me the look. He's either wishing I'd leave the house or wondering if I'd taste better with gravy.

Day 17 – Stocked up on 10 cans of tuna, 20 pounds. of rice, 5 boxes of Cheerios, and 36 eggs.

Day 18 – Realize I hate tuna, cereal, and eggs. And rice is gross.

Day 19 – Since when did vintage sports become a thing?

Day 20 – Decide to give *Tiger King* another try. Can't take my eyes off the ridiculousness. Joe Exotic must be lip-syncing.

Day 21 – If my husband talks about interest rate, GDP, or debt levels one more time, so help me God, I'm giving myself coronavirus.

Day 22 – Cutting my bangs with cellophane tape and the dullest scissors I own seemed like a good idea.

Day 23 – Remember the good ol' days when we used to argue about which way to hang the toilet paper?

Day 24 – Participated in second Zoom meeting with Toastmasters group.

Day 25 – Did you know that you can make your own licorice? You just need sweetened condensed milk and Himalayan pink sea salt…and unfortunately I have none of those items.

Day 26 – The only thing worse than your husband watching sports 24/7, is your husband watching vintage sports from 1998.

Day 27 – I realize that I am unable to take care of myself. I have no skills. I cannot cut hair, make butter, manufacture aluminum foil, set up Zoom, or build a thermometer.

Day 28 – Watching a plastic bag blow down the street and get caught in a rose bush. For one hour.

Day 29 – Husband sneezed directly inside the refrigerator. Is it too late to pick someone else to self-quarantine with?

Day 30 – Dropped off a can of Lysol to a friend for her birthday.

Day 31 – I have 125 freckles on my right arm and 73 on my left. Do I need to see a dermatologist?

Day 32 – Is the expiration date on canned food a recommendation, a suggestion, or a demand?

Day 33 – I don't even recognize myself on FaceTime.

Day 34 – What's better? Mashed, baked, fried or au gratin potatoes? Should I care?

Day 35 – Adult coloring books are bullshit.

Day 36 – I've forgotten the names of my favorite restaurants.

Day 37 – Literally don't remember how to drive a car. Is the little knob for the radio or the air conditioning? On the plus side, I still have a full tank of gas.

Day 38– Keeping track of the days with a marker on the wall like a prisoner. Day XXXVIII.

Day 39 and beyond – See Day 14

ANOTHER MILESTONE BIRTHDAY

by Katie Glauber Bush

Milestone birthdays have been a consistent problem in my life. The most recent celebrations include an ill-fated trip to Ireland for my 50th birthday, an overnight forest facial for my 60th, and a national let-grandma-die celebration for my special 70th coronavirus birthday.

Oprah was honored at a televised *fête* for her 50th. Demi jetted with friends to Dubai to celebrate hers. And when my 50th birthday loomed close, my friends and family asked how I wanted to celebrate it. I knew I had no interest in a massive party with all eyes focused on my half-century self. But European travel. Now that was something worth considering. My husband, Mike, and I chose a 16-day trip to England and Ireland. The Trafalgar tour day-by-day itinerary read like sensuous travel porn.

On June 21, we would celebrate my landmark birthday on the Ring of Kerry in western Ireland. Or, at least, that was the plan. Four missed flights, a run-in with Interpol agents ending in my husband being escorted off the plane, luggage lost for the duration of the trip leaving me attired in a blue jean jumper and gift shop t-shirt for two weeks, and finally, the loss of five of the fourteen tour days, all made it a little less special.

Turning 60 brought its own unique challenges. I have been six feet tall since I was twelve years old. I am not a small-boned woman. I wear my hair short and when a cashier is busy and fails to look up, I have even been called "sir." But I'm as womanly as any petite female you might know. So, you can imagine my horror when approaching the age of 60, I began to sport a fine, downy fuzz on my upper lip and chin line. As any postmenopausal woman can tell you, there is no joy in being a bearded lady unless you are earning money in a Barnum & Bailey sideshow. And I was not. Mexican artist Frida Kahlo created colorful, evocative, mustachioed self-portraits. I'm not sure from where Frida's self-confidence or bravado came, but I know that if I were talented enough to paint a self-portrait, I would lop off forty pounds and ditch the facial hair.

On the big day, I bought my first depilatory, dutifully read the instructions, and attacked my face with a scorched-earth attitude. My skin was burning, and my eyes were watering, but I persevered until every hair was gone. Happy birthday to me. I now sport a clean, smooth stiff upper lip (however, no matter my age, I choose not to address the hairy challenges of each year's bathing suit season).

This year, I will be 70 years old. In February, a talented orthopedist removed my brittle, broken down knee and replaced it with a superhero titanium model. During my third week of recovery, the governor of my state asked us to shelter safely at home due to Coronavirus. I was caught completely off guard. The joys of hydrocodone had kept the specter of a pandemic off my fuzzy mental radar. My anal-retentive tendencies and Martha Stewart abilities inspired me to stock up on pantry basics, paper goods and toiletries prior to my surgery. I began February confident that my husband and I would have most of what we needed for my six to eight weeks of recuperation.

How smug I sat, knowing I was the only woman in my subdivision with a cache of 48 rolls of toilet paper on my basement shelves. Toilet paper was only the first of the shortages. Next, you couldn't find a grain of rice in the entire state. A week or so later, someone robbed the henhouse because there wasn't an egg to be found. Meat shortages loomed on the horizon. How naïve and privileged I was to think this was the worst that would come.

Two months into the crisis, the president decided – since he'd run on making the economy great and it was now tanking – he would announce that he was "opening up the country again." Health officials weighed in with their concerns, if not dire warnings, that it was too soon and that a steep spike in coronavirus cases would be inevitable, especially in the vulnerable populations. A few of his colleagues convinced him to put it off for another month.

In an ingratiating suck that was heard around the world, the lieutenant governor of the great state of Texas went on FOX News to support our Commander-in-Chief. He declared to Tucker Carlson that people like him – grandparents in their twilight years – should risk death so people could stop social distancing and get back to work in order for the country to avert economic calamity. The network pundits' voices, supporting this opinion, flooded the FOX airwaves. The same political party that claimed to be so pro-life that they fought for years over one Florida woman on life support, now wanted to sacrifice grandma for the economy.

It was difficult not to take all this personally.

The bar came down and I was now locked in the seat of an emotional *coronacoaster*. Up and up the coaster climbed, as our governor announced the reopening of barber shops and hair salons.

Further skyward, as we were told it appeared to be safe for groups of ten or less to gather, if wearing masks and social distancing. Now, it was finally possible to see our grown children and grandkids.

Then, the coaster changed course—careening downward when word came that a few months earlier my local police, with a no-knock warrant, broke down the home door of Breonna Taylor, an innocent young black woman and emergency medical technician. They shot her dead. One week later, in another American city, a police officer held his knee down on the neck of George Floyd, a black man who was peacefully accepting his own arrest. The officer pressed his knee down for over eight deadly minutes.

My 70th birthday is in a few days. The country has begun to open for business again—exceptionally fast in some states and more slowly in others. Now, if we can just get our minds and hearts to open, as well. It remains to be seen which of the two diseases will be deadlier, take more victims, shatter more families—coronavirus or racism. When we overcome these diseases, that truly will be a milestone worthy to celebrate.

Surviving Quarantine

THE TP-ING POINT

by Bethany Grace Howe

As a former dude, it is not lost on me the privilege I used to have. I got paid more for doing the same amount of work as a woman. When I spoke in meetings other people shut up because I had an obnoxious, booming baritone that over-rode everyone else. I could pee behind trees when I was camping without a care in the world. Even if I got caught, I could just shrug and head back to make S'mores.

Four years later, if I'm being honest, not all of this has changed. Now unemployed in the wake of COVID-19, I am still making the same money as all the unemployed women I know. In meetings, I might even be more domineering. As I never changed my voice, and with everyone now being at least six feet away, my volume is a needed asset.

But to say my toilet paper habits have changed greatly is an under-statement. I used to be able to make a roll last for weeks. When I was a guy, assuming I was doing the bulk of my bathroom business at work or area coffee shops, I could make a roll last nearly a month. Now, I create enough empty toilet paper rolls that my daughter can make holiday poppers for every occasion Christian, Muslim, and Hallmark.

So it was that I arose at 6 a.m. last Sunday to prepare for the journey to my local Costco. Driving by it every day on my way home from the unemployment office, I know people start lining up there at 6:45 a.m. and I wanted to get my place in line.

Costco, if you have not been near one recently, currently looks like a fortress. With walls of carts cable-locked together now blocking the entrance, people are channeled into proper lanes that leave no chance for a rush on the doors. It's like lining up for Space Mountain but with fewer special effects and warnings to pregnant women.

I was the third one there, and very quickly one of the veterans of past Costco crusades let me know that we should line up with our carts already between us. Better for social distancing, as well as leaving you fully prepared to run over anyone who tries to cut in line.

Sitting there on the cold concrete with my blanket and my reading materials, I was fully prepared for whatever came next – except for what came next. "I'm sorry," said the nice Costco man arriving to work, "we're out of toilet paper."

I responded well to this. No, really.

For just last week when I was at Costco, I did not respond well to something. In fact, I was a complete raging bitch to someone who had the actual audacity to do her job. I felt bad enough then to go back and apologize, and as mad as I was now about the lack of toilet paper, it was not this employee's fault. Also, my ass was freezing.

Trudging back to the car, I decided that since I was up and interacting with asymptomatic people who might in five-to-14 days bring about my death, I should head for Safeway. Running out of kitty treats and now living with my cats full time, I am keenly aware at any time they are capable of nibbling off my toes when I'm asleep.

Once in Safeway, I found myself going where I always did lately: the cavernous space once known as the "paper goods aisle." I never find any toilet paper there, but I enjoy hearing my echo bounce off the shelves. What I saw this time, however, stopped me and my vagina in our tracks: Charmin. A whole 12-pack of it. Extra-strong, even. Gold, Xanadu, and Shangri-La, all wrapped up in plastic covered with bears that for some reason need clean underwear but are nevertheless always naked.

Looking about the aisle, I made sure I was alone. As predatory as I was becoming about my toilet paper needs, I recalled my descent into moral depravity earlier at Costco. I knew I was perfectly capable of steamrolling an elderly person or a yodeling child to serve my needs.

But the aisle was empty, and after making my purchase I made my way out of the store. Already other people were coming in, each of them side-eyeing me with that look that says, "We know where you live and how much toilet paper you now own."

Arriving at my car in the light of the new day, I thrust my purchase towards the rising sun and chanted the opening lines to *The Lion King*.

Really. People don't hassle you when they think you've lost your mind.

Driving home, I rejoiced in my conquest, thrilled that I achieved what others had not. I had beaten the hoarders, I had defied the Fortress at Costco. I was the victorious woman. I was the Amazon Prime-less Warrior who had come home with the prize. I was...I was in serious trouble.

I forgot the kitty treats.

SUBSTITUTIONS MADE BY YOUR INSTACART SHOPPER

by Courtney Watson

1. Spinach
Someone's feeling optimistic.

2. Almond milk
You won't drink this.

3. Oat milk
Or this.

4. Cashew milk
You know you don't have to pretend with me, right?

5. Whole milk, half gallon
There it is. Better make it a gallon. To go with the cookies.

6. Yogurt, Greek
How virtuous. I know you're hoping they'll be out and I'll substitute the one you flip the candy bits in. I got you, girl.

7. Carrots
If you insist.

8. Bananas

Has the last bunch rotted already?

9. Kale
Lol.

10. Rosehip Oil Conditioner
Again? Are you eating it? Because you're definitely not eating kale.

11. Mint Milanos.
Here. We. Go.

12. Duncan Hines Chewy Fudge Brownie Mix (2)
You complete me.

13. Duncan Hines Triple Chocolate Fudge Brownie Mix
Oh shit, did he dump you?

14. Cheetos
He dumped you during a pandemic?

15. Carlo Rossi Jug of Wine, Red
Did you know there are five bottles in a gallon of wine?

16. Carlo Rossi Jug of Wine, White
So I should probably get two.

17. Goody 6.5" Haircutting Scissors
Oh, hell no.

18. Frozen mozzarella sticks (3)
Hang tight. I'm on my way.

QUARANTINED IN THE KITCHEN

by Ariel Balter

My feminist credentials are quite impressive: a BA from a women's college, advanced degrees, I am a working parent, and a participant and activist in various women's causes, to name a few. While I care about the aesthetics of my home and like to eat good food and have high standards of cleanliness, I shun the role of domestic goddess, on principle.

Despite being raised by a mother who is a fine chef and hostess and having had grandmothers whose self-worth depended largely on feeding people hearty portions of homemade food, and keeping nice homes, I have refused to be the spouse who greets her husband with a roasted free-range chicken and organic vegetables when he returns from work. Nor do I ever volunteer to make healthy snacks for my daughter's school events. I am more than happy to eat out, order take out, and purchase prepared foods, and school lunches, but don't ask me to bake cupcakes for thirty children, ten gluten free, five ovo-lacto free, all nut-free, and absolutely no food coloring. Call someone else, preferably a dad.

Much as I hate to admit it, and due to my upbringing, I am a competent cook and baker. I was raised to get a Ph.D. and manage a home. I don't usually mind cooking or engaging in domesticity if it is of my own free will and providing that I do not appear to be enacting the role of a housewife. Never address me by that title. I also resent being asked to cook for others and the assumption that as a wife and mother, it is my role to do so. I'm the one who brings crackers and cheese or store-bought desserts to potluck dinners, rather than colorful, multi-ingredient salads spritzed with homemade dressings.

Against the advice of my daughter's preschool teachers, I did not spend the early years of my daughter's life baking with her, so that she could learn measurements and math. Despite my culinary negligence, she excels in math but isn't much of a baker or especially adept in the kitchen. While I hope that she will be self-sufficient, I don't want her perspiring over a hot stove on anyone else's behalf.

So given my hostility towards the domestic realm, how is it that while sheltering-in-place in the age of COVID-19, I find myself cooking at least three meals a day for three people, all of whom have different dietary needs and tastes, baking from scratch, experimenting with new recipes, discussing my concoctions with friends, and actually admitting this in public?! In the pre-Corona days, none of us ate lunch at home on weekdays. Now, I must accommodate my undomesticated omnivorous husband, who, by the way is allergic to eggs, my tween/scholar daughter who is too busy taking classes on Zoom to bother with the kitchen and who is a vegetarian, largely a pastafarian, and a picky eater, and of course myself.

The coronavirus pandemic has turned me into a 1950s housewife.

Since the lockdown I have subscribed to a weekly delivery of organic farm products, which arrive covered in dirt and dead insects (not to mention possible COVID-19 germs), so I have to scrub until my hands are raw. While living under the coronavirus regime, I now have a store-room filled with staples such as ten-pound bags of flour and sugar, and various oils, in addition to the mainstay we have always had on hand, dried pasta. Given the number of eggs two-thirds of us now consume, we should consider adopting some pet chickens.

Since the lockdown began, I have baked at least ten banana bread loaves, numerous other quick breads, homemade buttermilk waffles using a waffle iron that I received for my wedding nineteen years ago and haven't used much since then, attempted to make crepes—once successfully and a second time, less so, setting off the smoke alarm, baked tofu for my vegetarian daughter, despite the fact that I don't much care for the gelatinous soy product, and experimented with crispy kale, bok choy, and other vegetables I've avoided making over the years.

And I feel absolutely no sense of accomplishment or pride. In fact, I am ashamed to admit that I enter the kitchen to make anything other than toast and coffee or boil pasta.

I do have my limits, though. Under no circumstances will I participate in the sourdough epidemic that is sweeping our nation. I don't do yeast breads. They are far too time consuming and labor intensive. Though punching and aggressively kneading a mound of dough might be therapeutic at this time. And unless the bacterial starter, propagating spores that need to fester for weeks in order to develop into sourdough bread, proves to be a cure for COVID-19, I don't want any cultures growing in my kitchen.

I tell myself that at least I am still maintaining some small sense of dignity by confining myself to relatively easy and quick cooking projects. Since the advent of coronavirus, in my regular texts with a group of female friends, for the first time in our years of friendship, we have been discussing and exchanging recipes, including photos and links to various cooking websites. These are a group of smart, educated, professional, independent women who now see fit to contemplate the best crepe pans and "clean" recipes, whatever that is, alongside analyses of articles in *The New Yorker* and scientific journals.

Perhaps to support my developing, corona-induced wine-drinking habit, I should learn to make wine. I live in California after all. Then I can benefit from the fruit of my labors and become oblivious to or even revel in my time spent in the kitchen. Stomping on grapes would allow me to vent, and fermented "foods" are salubrious. That's a "cooking" project I might be able to get on board with. Or more likely, next, I will attempt a key lime pie since I received a substantial sack of limes in the farm delivery and don't know what else to do with them.

Of late, I have taken to decorating or personifying and animating the excess or unappealing produce in our coffers and displaying our fruit and vegetable friends on a plate in the kitchen. I've poked them with chopsticks, inserting them as antennae, and fashioned legs made of corn cob holders, used stickers and permanent markers for facial features, and constructed origami hats for them. I must be taking out my aggressions on our food or am losing my mind. Clearly the domestic and culinary life is not for me.

Please contact a mental health professional if I start making sourdough bread.

MOTHER EARTH: IT'S NOT QUARANTINE — IT'S TIME OUT FOR BAD CHILDREN

by Leigh Anne Jasheway

How are you enjoying time-out, children? Not so much? Well, boo-fucking-hoo.

I told you to settle down. I warned you that if you didn't clean your oceans and start treating each other better, there would be consequences. But you didn't listen. So I sent fire, I sent hurricanes, I sent another unwatchable season of *Survivor: Earth*, but still, you ignored your Mother like you ignore those signs in public bathrooms that tell you to wash your damn hands after you tinkle.

(I saw that eye roll! Just for that, you're grounded for another two months!)

You're listening now, right? I finally got your attention with a virus. I did NOT want to go there, but I had no choice. You thought I was bluffing? Now that you can't hang out with your friends or poop freely because you're afraid you might run out of toilet paper, are you finally ready to give me the respect I deserve?

(Don't scowl at me behind that face mask. I can see your forehead furrow.)

What's that? You're sorry? Really? That's the best you've got? Like when you were sorry for spilling gasoline and blaming everything on plastic straws or wasting energy watching internet porn and trying to pass it off as sociology homework? You apologize to me almost as often as a homophobic politician does to his wife after having been caught having an affair with a 19-year-old guy he met on Grindr. And just as believably.

Like handshakes and open-mouth kissing strangers in a bar, the time for apologies is over.

Instead, I've come up with a list of chores that I expect you to do to gain my trust enough so that I will let you have your freedom again. **Consider these chores my Earth Day gift** (and remember, every day is Earth Day from here on out). You were planning to get me a gift, right? And not one of those silly "coupon" books filled with things that cost you nothing, like "I'll put up those solar panels this summer when there's no football to watch" or "I promise not to raise tigers at home."

Here is the list of things I expect from you if you want to be ungrounded any time in the near future:

Take out the trash. Not only do I expect you to sort the garbage into recyclables and non, before hauling it to the curb every week, I expect you to vote every science-denying, Mother Earth-destroying mofo out of office. (This mo is tired of being fo'ed!) Don't just vote during presidential election years, but every year there is any kind of election from here forward—I don't care if it's an election for county cat communicator. If people in Wisconsin can vote during a pandemic, you sure as hell can vote when it's your turn.

Be kind to your neighbors. You know those people next door you don't really like because they play country music or never close their blinds when they have naked dance parties in the evening? Be kind to them. They might have hand-sanitizer! Or batteries for your vibrator! But even if they can't do anything for you, be kind to ALL your neighbors. The bees, the earthworms, the cows, the pigs, the big ol' owls who freak you out because they remind you of your math teacher in the 8th grade who gleefully insisted you solve story problems before you could go to lunch. Don't harm anyone unless you have no other choice. Do I have to keep "accidentally" starting pandemics that jump from animals to humans to drill this message into your head?

Do less. This seems easier now, right? Since you've been grounded, you're driving less and spending less time mindlessly shopping for things you don't need. See how much fun it can be to pay attention to the people and things and articles of clothing that make good face masks you already have in your life? Who knew? Mama knew that's who!

Stop wasting food. If I've told you once, I've told you 7.8 billion times, there are hungry people in the world who will not turn up their noses at my chickpea and quinoa salad because "it tastes funny." I'm hoping this is a lesson you're learning during your time-out when shopping for groceries is like a game of real-life *Survivor* and sometimes you have to make do with what's in your pantry and fridge, even if that is half a cup of oatmeal and a limp cucumber. Get creative. Eat it all. And remember: There are people somewhere eating toilet paper tonight because they spent all their money on that instead of food.

Put your money where your heart is. It's time to stop buying things from companies that think trashing my turf is dandy as long as there's a profit in it. Spend your money wisely and avoid those who rape and pillage (I'm looking at you, Nestle, Coca-Cola, Monsanto, Kraft, Bank of America, Procter & Gamble, Koch Industries, Exxon, Chevron, Shell, Harvey Weinstein... Don't make me stop this electric car and look at me when I'm talking to you!)

Never, ever take a cruise. Jeez, you would have thought food poisoning and Legionnaire's Disease would have taught you that lesson years ago, but no, you kept hopping aboard, thinking you'd find love or at least alcoholism at sea. Meanwhile the *Shitshow of the Sea* or whatever she's called, has continued to destroy the only place marine life has to call home. Why do you think it's called "grounded"?

So, that's what I want. No. That's what I <u>need </u>from you. You make good on this list and I will let you go play with your friends again. Deal?

Remember: I will outlive you, so watch your step!

GROCERY STORE BATTLE

by Jennifer Scully

Who knew that the biggest risk of an apocalypse was love handles? When I imagined myself in the midst of an apocalypse, I pictured some version of Tina Turner in *Thunderdome* mixed with *Xena: Warrior Princess*—custom leather, bow and arrow, and the physique of a badass. Instead, I've become *Jen: Recliner Princess*—spandex, remote control, and the physique of a lard-ass. I need to get back to healthier eating; even spandex has its limits.

I've discovered that the best way to lose weight is to read diet blogs online—by the time you've finished them you're too tired to cook and you've lost your appetite. All of the blogs follow the same, miserable format. There is the mandatory opening, explaining the long family tradition that somehow inspired you to make a very non-traditional recipe: "When I was knee-high to a grasshopper growing up on a farm, I used to sit on the porch with my grandma watching the cows chewing grass in the field. Eating my recipe for nonfat dehydrated kale chips takes me right back to the farm, like a cow chewing her cud."

Next, the blogger is required to talk about how convenient the recipe is, because they are such a busy person: "Now that I'm a busy mom/prospective American Ninja Warrior/astronaut, I just don't have much time to make organic meals from scratch for my 10 children/herd of goats/pet leprechauns/7 dwarves. Even Grumpy, my pickiest eater, loves these nonfat dehydrated kale chips and asks for seconds!"

And then there are the notes: "You can use store-bought ingredients, but your food will taste like the sadness of your own laziness. And in fact, I not only like to make everything homemade, I prefer to hand forge all of my own pots, pans, and cooking utensils in a foundry I've built in my garage, but, if you really have to, you can use store-bought equipment."

But nothing is as terrible as a keto blog. How do you know someone is on the keto diet? Don't worry, they'll tell you. The keto religion has pervaded the online recipe world like missionaries with smallpox. You could also call this diet "A Thousand Ways to Eat an Avocado with Bacon." I'm a nutritional atheist and avoid keto sites like the plague, but sometimes I come across them by mistake, like when you're humming along to a great new song on the radio and then realize you've accidentally been listening to Christian Rock.

And then there are the sites that try to make healthy foods into the shape of unhealthy foods. Can't eat pizza? We've mashed up some soupy cauliflower and put it in a pizza pan and called it a pizza crust! We've taken squishy squashes and reformulated them into the shape of spaghetti noodles! We've mashed chickpeas and formed them into the shape of an ice cream cone! Unfortunately, people actually expect others to eat these foods, not just look at a picture of them. Just because you form a vegetable into the shape of a noodle doesn't make it a noodle. It's an...impasta. I could shape a turd into a circle and it doesn't make it a cookie.

And finally, finally, you make it far enough through the blog to get to the actual recipe. You've been this blogger's captive audience, scrolling through pages of useless information, plus three ads inspired by your unfortunate internet search for "Does a platypus have a penis?" After all of that reading, the recipe says something like: "Take kale, microwave for 2 minutes, allow enough time to come to terms with your life choices that brought you to this moment, and enjoy!" How good can a recipe be if you explicitly have to ask someone to enjoy it? "I know these kale chips taste like the leaves that fell out of the salad bag a few months ago in the back of the refrigerator, but really, I command you to ENJOY THEM!! IT IS A REQUIRED PART OF THE RECIPE! Well, fuck you, Marianne. You and your kale recipe are not the boss of me.

I'll enjoy them if I want to. Right after I read this recipe about broccoli that has been reformulated into the shape of a brownie.

PANDEMIC LOCKDOWN:
IT'S BETTER THAN AN IRANIAN PRISON CELL

by Jasmine Eftekhari

In Iran, we have been in quarantine to fight COVID-19 for three months. Or is it three years? It's so hard to tell now that the days all run together. Every day seems to be *Mondathursday*.

I recently got a chance to speak with friends in other countries and for a while, I felt that what we are all going through has brought us closer, made us feel united, and shown us how much we have in common, like weight gain and wishing our children would let us go to the bathroom in peace. Most of the people in the world dream of being able to go outside without a mask, hold their loved ones by the hand, and hug random strangers who may or may not run away. For a few minutes, during our conversation, I was reminded that we all live on the same planet.

But our conversation also highlighted how different our lives are, depending upon where in the world we live.

For example, for us in Iran, it is completely normal to feel as if we were already in a cage—we have restrictions and limits on every aspect of our lives from the day we are born, so this quarantine isn't as big of a disruption to our daily lives. I'm not saying this is a good thing, but it is easier to adjust to lockdown when you've never really tasted freedom. On the other hand, I keep seeing and reading about people who are used to certain freedom, going wild with outrage, protesting in the streets for things they consider necessities—haircuts, tattoos, and drinking somewhere other than home. And, apparently, in places like America, going shopping at the mall is more important than being alive.

Are they for real?

Here in Iran, we had to work hard through social campaigns to force the Iranian government to put us in quarantine after we passed a 20% mortality rate. We like living; we're weird like that. Also, it doesn't matter how unruly our hair is when we women hide it under a hijab.

For Americans and others, restrictions on freedom are a new experience, something that they couldn't even fathom. Stopping their normal lives for something they don't have any control over. And after a couple of weeks, some of them decided they were as mad as hell and they just weren't going to take it anymore! Apparently, like yogurt, their ability to self-isolate has a short expiration date. The idea that quarantine would last for another month or longer is just unacceptable to them, and no amount of banana bread and boxed wine is going to change that.

For these freedom-loving folks, being locked up at home is an unpleasant and stressful experience. For me, however, it is quite the opposite. Because in my opinion, being locked in my house is a thousand times better than being locked in a cell of an Iranian jail for some stupid political accusations such as having written on social media that "Women must have the right to choose how to dress."

Having the opportunity to connect with the outside world, to talk about this quarantine with friends (or even a doctor or a psychiatrist), to call your parents and listen to their voices, to know that you can eat whenever you want, to watch TV, see the live reports of real or fake news on social media—these are all miracles for those who have spent even just a week in jail. Trust me, I know.

So, I appreciate spending all my time at home with my daughter, watching her wake up, play, smile, and grow. It sure beats being in a 2x2 meter room with five other women and worrying about your child at home without you.

At least, I did appreciate my time with my daughter for the first two or three weeks of the quarantine. You see, she is 3 years old and seems to be fueled by the same enriched uranium the Iranian regime uses for their famous "atomic bombs." She never gets tired! After ten days of being locked in the house with her, I started to think that no torture could ever be more deadly than spending 24 hours together without a break At least the women I had shared a cell with didn't whine: "Mommy!

Mommy! Mommy!" at me every waking hour.

Now I am posting against the Iranian government on all my social media accounts, signed with my first and last name, just to be noticed and read by the regime's secret services. I condemn the Iranian politicians for how they managed the whole COVID-19 situation, for all their lies about the numbers of infected and dead people in recent months. I tell everyone to go to hell, just so I can be arrested and taken to jail. But they're ignoring me. Who knew the Iranian government would ghost a former prisoner? I'm ready to video-stream live on Instagram in partnership with some American feminists just to be considered dangerous for national security and to be taken away from home.

If nothing else works, I will use the advice that the wise President Trump gave to all of us: I will inject myself with bleach and this nightmare will end.

HOMELESSNESS, QUEER KIDS AND COVID-19

by Belinda Carroll

All at once, a blur of short-cropped burgundy hair, short shorts and dark skin come whirling at me. Speaking in the droll seen-it-all tone of an experienced Queen twice her age, she says, "Heeeey, I'm Hailey." Looking down she grandly gestures toward her chest. "And these are my new bwwoooooobs" She draws out boobs as if the word has 12 syllables.

She was meaning to shock me, but I loved it. "Not shabby for washcloths!" I say back, giving her light shade. Her chest was created out of the washcloths we give out in the front lobby. She grins, looks me up and down appraising me, "Aiiiiii!" She sings as she swings around and flounces off. I laugh, and I am grateful for the laugh.

It was a hope that working to support the queer houseless community during the unprecedented COVID-19 pandemic would get my mind off of the fact that my life had completely collapsed as I knew it, and perhaps create some light moments in the middle of the dark moments I knew were sure to come.

Life had changed so much in the last few weeks that I felt like I was suddenly the protagonist in a Great Russian Novel. Within days of the shutdowns, I went from being a full-time comedian, producer and "sleep 'til nooner" to serving meals, turning over beds, explaining why we were out of meat options and sneaking a guest an extra cookie at dinner. I'm a punk rock Mom.

Years ago, I was houseless. I had come out as lesbian to a less-than-welcoming family. In 1992, the atmosphere wasn't ideal for queer people and many people got kicked out or lived in such toxic environments they had to leave.

My stint on the streets (1993-1996) was punctuated with staying on people's couches, in garages, in the City Nightclub's greenroom, under davenports and a few times in an unoccupied barn.

There weren't a ton of options for youth. I stayed at the downtown Greenhouse Salvation Army shelter once. They had (and have) anti-LGBTQ policies, and it came down through other street kids that the other gay kids weren't staying there. It wasn't safe for us.

That's why when the stay-at-home order was put in place and I got the opportunity to work at the emergency distancing shelter, I took it. Among other reasons, I knew how unhinged I felt during relatively a normal time in the world while dealing with houselessness. Dealing with houselessness now that everything was shut down would be an extra special kind of hell.

Humor in crisis is my jam. Make your childhood work for you, I always say.

If you ever want to know the resilience of people, work at a shelter. I'm not saying that as a pandering one-off. The stories will break your heart and make you wonder why, in this country of wealth, a country where our billionaires have reportedly made money during all of this, why we have people who don't have access to a basic roof and walls.

The population of the shelter runs the absolute gamut. From the chronically homeless to the people who just have become houseless since the pandemic began. We've got people who have previously owned homes, queer people, a couple of deaf folks, a former monk. About 40% are employed at or close to full-time and are trying to save up enough to gain permanent housing.

Most are trying their best, and some are fighting demons many people can't imagine, or can imagine and have fought themselves. They are colorful people who write, sing, paint, and do comedy.

So we started a variety open mic. Every week, we socially distance in the cafeteria, I host and people present poetry or sing karaoke or perform comedy. It's a small way for us to hold space to process, hear each other and make sense of the world.

Performing is the only way I've ever known how to find that in my life. Well, performance, weed, and cookies. Which explains 90% of my life decisions.

My assumption is we're going to be living like this for a hot minute, we need to have each other's backs, and find strength.

The hope is that this period creates the change we need, we succeed in defunding the police, we work on change where we are and where we can, and that we create a more equitable world worth emerging back into.

THE LONDON FLU

by Rochelle Asquith

Every three weeks of lockdown, UK Prime Minister Boris Johnson has been giving updates about what's going on, what's going to happen, all that stuff. So far, it's all been fairly predictable; buzz words have spread like, well, the flu. *Stay home, protect the NHS, save lives. Stay home, protect the NHS, save lives.* I hear it as I drift off to sleep. Last week, Boris changed it to *Stay alert*, which means 12,679,473 different things (approximately).

I've taken to yelling it at my unwilling family members. At least I have a captive audience, if you know what I mean. "Stay alert!" I cry, as they butter a slice of toast, which then ends up on the floor because I've startled them. I suppose it's their own fault - they weren't staying alert like Boris told us to.

On the 11th March, Boris announced that you can now go to someone's house, as long as you're being paid, which follows absolutely no logic, and has no precedent whatsoever. Will the transfer of cash somehow stop the spread of the virus? That's what Boris seems to think. You can have your cleaner come in, but you can't see your family. My sister actually paid me thirty pounds to do her dishes once. Technically, we wouldn't be breaking the rules if we did that again.

Politicians in Scotland, Wales, and Northern Ireland have all come forward to say, "Don't listen to Boris, he's talking shite again," in a wonderful display of unity (if you can call it that). At least some of the UK is actually united in something, even if it is in disdain against the other part. So, I suppose not that much has changed.

Lockdown has meant many of us are realizing certain things for the first time. For example, I've really come to terms with the fact that you can add "if you know what I mean" onto basically any sentence and it will immediately imply extra meaning that leaves the recipient usually quite uncomfortable. For example, "I like to swing the ol' sack of drills, if you know what I mean."

When lockdown was first announced, the world seemed to split in two: introverts, despite the obvious bad-ness of the whole thing, were actually looking forward to having a cast-iron excuse to not go out. And extroverts who have had their whole worlds turned upside down and aren't allowed to swing the ol' sack of drills anymore, if you know what I mean. Through lockdown so far (at the time of writing, obviously), I've read seven books, mainly because there are so many books on my shelves that would never forgive me if I didn't read them now. I can't use the excuse that I don't have the time, not since that guy ate that bat. Or was it a pangolin? Who cares?

With all that reading under my belt, I think I can say that lockdown for me has been strangely productive. Like many people, I've been looking back at past plagues and attempting to string out some sort of narrative out of this whole thing. If this period of history will follow the Joseph Campbell Hero's Journey model, we're at the second trial part, just before the massive victory. Problematically, this trial could last a very long time. And it could involve a dragon or two, though that is slightly less likely, even despite the insanity of current news cycles.

When the Black Death was kicking about, people back then didn't have anything like Netflix or Just Eat. They had to rely on carrier pigeons, or if Harry Potter's not made up, owls. I can't imagine doing lockdown without modern technology - particularly Facetime. Although sending notes via bird-mail to a significant other, wouldn't be all that different from Tinder. If the history books have taught us anything, it's that humans are, and have always been pretty much the same. Men have always said, "Haha, without me?" when you tell them you're doing literally anything. At least most of us in the Western side of the world don't live in houses made of dung and mud like they did in the olden times.

Another advantage of living in today's plague is that we have face masks that aren't as cumbersome as those big beak things that doctors during the Black Plague used to wear. They were awful, and I'm pretty sure people weren't flogging them on Facebook back then. I googled the

Black Death to figure out how they beat it, and it turns out it was by quarantining, so that's great news for every country who's not really bothering with the whole quarantine thing.

It doesn't matter if you're an extrovert or an introvert, an outie or an innie. I suppose we're all learning from each other in these *shudders* unprecedented times, figuring it all out as we go. Thank god it's just a pandemic, and we don't have to worry about climate change or important elections, or EU negotiations or anything like that, am I right? Just keep swinging the ol' sack of drills, if you know what I mean.

ADVICE FOR SURVIVING LOCKDOWN FROM THE *MISS CONGENIALITY* MOVIES

by Leigh Anne Jasheway

Sometimes binge-watching old movies for hours at a time without leaving the sofa even when there's a pot-full of quinoa burning on the stove isn't unadulterated laziness. It's education, pure and simple (with an emphasis on the simple). Besides, smoky quinoa is probably going to be the next trending food on *Food Network*.

Case in point—I just watched *Miss Congeniality* and *Miss Congeniality 2: Armed and Fabulous* back-to-back and I've applied lessons learned from these movies for getting through social distancing/self-quarantine/house arrest.

Just look at all these great tips:

"Now if you'll excuse me, I have to go unscrew my smile!"
Sandra Bullock's character Gracie Hart teaches us that while sometimes you may have to put on a happy face to make sure the rest of the family (or your coworkers or the pack of wild hyenas you adopted right before everything went to shit) stays happy, it is just as important for you to stop pretending that everything is alright. It's called "resting" bitch face for a reason. We're resting!

"Eyebrows – there should be two!"
In the original movie, Victor Melling (played by Michael Caine) tries to

whip Gracie into shape for the beauty pageant, presenting her with lots of advice, including the above quote that can serve as a low bar standard in our approach to quarantine beauty regimens. It's absolutely fine to go a week without showering (as long as no one in the family starts spraying you with Lysol every time you near them) or stop shaving your legs until we've voted in a new president and gotten a handle on everything, pandemic or otherwise. But when you've reached unibrow status, you've probably sunk too low.

"You might consider a Tic-Tac."
While there's no real harm in neglecting a lot of personal hygiene activities, daily dental hygiene is vital. If you stop brushing and flossing for a week, you're going to pay the price. And by "price," I don't mean your dental co-pay because who knows how long it will be before you trust someone in a mask to put their gloved hands in your mouth (calm down, kinksters). If you don't take care of your teeth now, you're going to find yourself doing your own drilling and filling with Phillips' screwdriver and a soldering iron. And who's got laughing gas just lying around the house? (If you do, please tell me. These margaritas are no longer doing the job!)

"Rule #1, no hitting. Rule #2, chew with your mouth closed. Rule #3, no snorting."
Just as Joel Meyers, played by Diedrich Bader, lays down the rules in *Miss Congeniality 2*, it's important to set boundaries for the people you are spending 24/7 with (even if those "people" are the voices in your head). If you keep pushing each other's buttons while you're stuck inside together for a few months, marriage counselors and divorce lawyers are gonna have a field day when we can all finally fly the coop. You know what they say, "Families that set boundaries together, stay together. At least until they're allowed to take separate cars again."

"Gracie: I'd also like one of those little muffins."
"Sam: Where would you like it?"
Chances are, if you're a woman with a spouse, boyfriend, children, pack of hyenas sharing your space, you may find yourself falling into the stereotypical role of "housewife," what with the cooking, the serving, the cleaning, the wearing pearls and 5-inch stiletto heels while ordering Alexa to tell Roomba to sweep the floors and bring you a martini. But if

you listen to FBI agent Sam Fuller (played by Regina King in *Miss Congeniality 2*), you'll hear an important message about putting your own needs first. And also, reminding others to stick things where the sun don't shine if they get in the way of your self-care.

"I would so like to hurt you right now."
During these troubling times (to quote every commercial on TV right now reminding us that we need to stay home but also buy as many things as possible), it's important to feel your feelings. But it's also important to understand that you can't act on all of them. This is where something like Dammit Dolls come in handy. These dolls are meant to get the stuffing whacked out of them, so you don't end up in prison. You can find these online. If you're crafty and tired of making face masks for your neighbors, you can also sew your own voodoo dolls, but I'm not sure having sharp pins readily at hand is advisable.

"Miss Rhode Island, please describe your idea of a perfect date."
"That's a tough one. I would have to say April 25th. Because it's not too hot, not too cold, all you need is a light jacket."
Thanks to Miss Rhode Island for reminding us that it's okay to be confused, both about language and time. Without looking at a calendar, can you say with certainty what day it is? What month even? We're all discombobulated (and yes, I'm totally having an extra Margarita for remembering a word that long) right now, so cut yourself a lot of slack.

"Whatever happened to World Peace?"
"It comes and goes."
Goals change. Sometimes you're marching in the streets with millions of women for peace and justice and sometimes you're marching into the kitchen wondering how you're going to be able to make dinner for four out of a half box of Cheerios, diet Dr. Pepper, and a tub of Sabra Hummus. Right now, most of us are probably doing the latter, but when you get a few minutes between slamming a Dammit Doll and flossing, consider doing something to help make the world a better place, no matter how small the effort seems right now.

Last, but not least, don't judge yourself for watching all the movies and TV you want. You're not lazy; you're earning your Ph.D. in Netflixology.

GROCERY STORE BATTLE – DID I MENTION THAT I AM CHINESE-AMERICAN?

by Christina Tang-Bernas

I ready myself for battle. I check my purse for all the essentials:

1. Cloth facemask (washed yesterday with soap and hot water, imported from South Korea from my favorite local children's store, pale denim blue because it matches almost any outfit).
2. Spray hand sanitizer (scented with lavender and tea tree oil, purchased online from my favorite indie makeup shop).
3. Nitrile gloves (bright hospital blue, gifted from my favorite mother-in-law, a retired nurse who has fully stocked us with medical supplies to last the next decade).
4. A single credit card and my driver's license (to avoid cross-contamination).
5. Extra fabric bags (our local Walmart grocery is still allowing us to bring our own bags because we bag our own groceries anyways).

I do one final check of the refrigerator and cabinets, adding items to the list app on my phone and asking my husband if he wants anything else.

As I go forth to re-supply our rapidly emptying pantry, my husband's task is to watch our toddler daughter.

When coronavirus first hit us in California, my husband was deemed an essential worker. In the midst of a major project, he was not allowed to work from home, so I had to take my daughter to the grocery store with me. My daughter has picked up this random habit of coughing when she is mad about something. This was pre-face mask-era, so there we were, in the midst of the grocery store, with my daughter coughing loudly and derisively because I had not allowed her to "help" me bag the apples.

Did I mention that I am Chinese-American? And my daughter looks quite a lot like me.

"Oh, stop *fake* coughing," I would say in the nicest mom voice I could muster. "That's so silly of you" [insert awkward laughter and quickly push my cart in a random direction].

Now that my husband has been given permission to intermittently work from home, I time all my grocery store visits so I can leave my daughter at home with him.

We trade risks. He risks the virus when he goes to work. And I risk it going to the grocery store.

In the parking lot, I don the face mask and gloves like armor. My eyes or nose or both always start itching the moment I tell myself I can't touch my own face. When I breathe too hard, I regret forgetting to brush my teeth in the morning.

Grabbing a cart, I swing into action. There is a fine line between making sure we are stocked with enough essentials to minimize the number of grocery visits and becoming a full-fledged hoarder. I deliberate over the oatmeal. I contemplate the milk. I mutter to myself over whether or not I really need another box of chocolate chip cookies.

I remember the initial panic of the shutdown in Los Angeles and Orange County. I remember my own panic when I could not find milk in three different grocery stores, right when my daughter had decided that milk was her favorite thing ever and wanted to drink twice as much as usual. I would've taken 2% milk. I would've taken that lactose-intolerant milk. I seriously even considered taking the skim milk if there had been any. The store shelves had been emptied of oatmeal, of eggs, and even (the horror!) rice. I remember calculating if I had enough sanitary pads at home to last through the next month while staring at the nothingness stretching out before me. None of the dystopian teen dramas I've watched has ever prepared me for people panic-buying dry cat food and pads.

The image of these empty shelves still haunts me.

My husband has been very understanding of the pantry currently overflowing with canned corn and dry spaghetti. He nods and says nothing when I show up with another gallon of milk, even though we already have an unopened one and one that's still half full (plus my backup milk stashed in the freezer taking up precious room). Most of all, he has been careful not to mention anything about all the boxes of chocolate chip cookies.

So now I navigate each aisle analyzing each product based on necessity, shelf life, and the likelihood it will disappear right when I run out at home.

All the while, I try not to make eye contact with anyone else. I swallow down any hint of a dry throat cough or a sniffle from allergies. I am excruciatingly polite and friendly. I do not take more than two of anything, even if there is no sign telling me that the items are limited. I am the haute couture of a model minority.

We had spent years living in cities with an Asian minority, where my husband and I were often one of the few if not only ethnically Asians in restaurants or at neighborhood events. We are used to the side-eyed looks and mostly-genial questions of where we were from (I was born in the United States, which often disappoints people expecting something more exotic, and devolves into lots of throat-clearing and "Well, what I meant was..." follow-up questions). Most of the time, however, it didn't make a huge difference to our day-to-day life.

But as COVID-19 began its inexorable march across the world map, it became very apparent that a lot of people forgot that for Chinese-Americans, "Chinese" is the adjective modifying the noun "Americans" instead of the other way around.

My family hasn't visited China in years, the last time as part of a tour group otherwise made up of one Hispanic family from Texas and a bunch of elderly white Americans. I can speak approximately kindergarten-level Mandarin Chinese (and have had Chinese shopkeepers make fun of my "American accent"), and now my fellow Chinese-Americans and I have ended up in the unenviable position of representing and defending an entire nation of which we have little to no connection with because of the way we look.

A girl I know was harassed at a grocery store while helping an elderly Chinese couple. In the comments of her Facebook post, someone commented that he purchased pepper spray for his parents for when they go grocery shopping. I have been asked, both jokingly and not-so-jokingly, why Chinese people eat such weird things (insert awkward laugh).

Our local Walmart grocery only carries one kind of tofu (not the kind I want, but the kind I settle for). I contemplate the single brand of sesame oil. In small letters, it says, "an Oriental Seasoning Oil." I have never purchased sesame oil that had to explain what its purpose was before. It is also three times the price I would usually pay, but I have not been able to summon the energy to go to the usual Chinese or Korean supermarkets, much further away than the 3-minute drive to this grocery store. I desperately miss dim sum and egg tarts and beef noodle soup that only tastes right dining in the restaurant. I place the small glass bottle in my cart.

By the time I check out, I am exhausted. My right eye has started to twitch, it's so itchy. I have a headache because breathing while wearing my mask keeps fogging up my glasses. My cheeks ache from maintaining a pleasant expression.

I take off my gloves in the car and spray my hands with sanitizer. It's redundant, but it makes me feel better (and smells lovely).

I am triumphant from another victory.

My husband comes outside to help me bring in the groceries.

"Wow," he says. "You got a lot."

I nod. "Hopefully this will tide us over for two weeks."

A week later, I'm gearing up again. My daughter has decided that she adores mandarin oranges and has devoured an entire 5 lb. bag in five days. My husband waves as once more, I go forth onto the field of battle.

I'M NOT READY TO DIE

by Linda White

During this epidemic, there is a political movement afoot to undermine the rights of certain members of society. Namely, old women. If that segment of the population disappeared, so what? Older women aren't important to anyone, according to some. I have to say I am incensed that I have been labeled detritus and could be relegated to society's dumping spot. I'm not about to be silenced. Senior women don't spend their time painting pale watercolors, writing insipid poetry, or knitting cardigans no one is going to wear. We've raised children, stepped in to help with grandchildren—and as volunteers, greased the wheels of community, to keep things rolling along.

"Wear out the old things first," we'd tease my mom when she was alive. It was meant as a joke. When she was tired out and it was her time, she passed on and I miss her every day. Now it seems we're not so concerned about wearing people out. They have a restricted usefulness and time limited stay on earth. Last time I checked, I didn't have an expiration date stamped anywhere on my body.

So when is someone worn out and ready for disposal? COVID-19 imposes a new reality on us all. The economy teeters on the edge of ruin, people lose their jobs, and kids can't go to school. Everyone looks like time travelers from the '70s: out-of-control hair, ragged fingernails, and unpainted toenails. Why waste valuable and rapidly depleting resources on someone whose "best before" date is past? Someone who is no longer a contributing member of society? Someone suffering dementia? Get rid of grandma! She's a drain on us all and no longer much to look at.

A precedent exists. "Granny dumping" solves the burden of a worn-out grandmother. When she needs 24-hour aid and is too demanding, families "drop her off." A family member claims to have found the old gal wandering around in the street, takes her to the emergency room, and abandons her. She might be in a wheelchair or walker, but she's lost and now the hospital's responsibility. No purse, no wallet. And voilà! The family isn't heard from again and the Granny problem is solved.

The obvious next step is to have her die. COVID-19 is a problem with its own solution. Granny gets the virus? Let nature take its course. One less mouth to feed, one less person to weigh down society. The young may also get sick, but think of the recovery celebrations they could have.

But this still leaves us with a problem. What do we do with Granny's body? Someone has to dispose of it and it has to be done safely. This virus will leave us with a bunch of dead old women piling up on the streets or in unmarked graves. Besides the unsightly mess and odor, the virus could be a health risk to the young and interfere with their parties.

The 1973 movie, *Soylent Green*, foresaw a similar problem. Like COVID-19, the dilemma of accumulating bodies might be its own solution. In the film, coincidentally set in New York, overpopulation, starvation, and a decimated planet, has led to societal breakdown. There are riots for food and the main supply for the masses is Soylent Red and Soylent Yellow, prepared from soy and lentils. A new product Soylent Green, made from ocean algae appears on the market, is tastier and more nutritious than the old varieties. Without providing more of the plot, it turns out, "Soylent Green is made of people."

This means that the old grannies could be recycled and put to a final good use. If the idea was spun the right way, most of the population would buy into it. People could snack away on *Granny Crunches*, *Granny Nibbles*, even *Granny Jerky*. There would be new jobs in meat preparation, new jobs in processing and packaging. Advertising and marketing companies would flourish.

Legislators have decisions to make. When is an old harridan ready for recycling? Are there historical clues or perhaps an online survey for relatives that would work? A list of 5 or so simple, yet cogent, questions that would determine when to turn Granny over. How many times has she told the same boring story? Does she run through every sibling's name before getting to yours? Did she give you socks for Christmas *again?* Does she think we're all headed to hell in a handbasket? There should, of course, be a finder's fee or donor's dividend.

"Let Granny Die."

An extreme solution? All atrocities begin wobbling at the top of a slippery slope. It's only a small slide from neglecting old women in continuing care to sending them out into the streets without masks or hand sanitizer and having them take their chances in the pandemic.

80% of COVID-19 deaths are among the elderly and the majority of them are women. Should we be rounding women aged 60 and over up, then discreetly disposing of them? The lockdown would be lifted. Bars, clubs, and restaurants—the whole of society could go back to "normal." Who doesn't want that?

I am not, in the words of my aunt Mary Storey, "Ready to snuff it yet." I am not ready to sacrifice myself. I am quite agile, my brain isn't too fried, and I do still contribute to society. I am vocal and loud. When I don't agree with something, everyone knows. The epitaph on my tombstone will be: "She had an opinion on everything and wasn't afraid to share it." I am insulted at the idea of dumping Granny. I'll speak out against granicide, and if that doesn't work, I'm not afraid to resort to revolution. We don't have to snuff Grannies. There are more deserving groups You know who you are.

CONTRIBUTORS

Silvia Bajardi As an Italian landed in the New World, she realized that "having the syndrome" was a constant for all women around the globe. She tried to cure it by founding *The Syndrome Mag* organization, and overcame her imposter syndrome by declaring herself: "The Directress."

Aaesha A. was born in Hinsdale, Illinois, and moved as a young child from one country to another, internalizing the nuances, people, and prejudices of each place. She graduated from high school in New Jersey, then moved to California, where she spent years studying people and the human mind. The Bay Area has since been her home where she writes to heal herself first, then others—especially those like herself who are struggling to find their place in the world—and lives with her husband, three children, two pets, and her coffee cup.

Rochelle Asquith is a writer, artist and avid reader from West Yorkshire, UK.

Ariel Balter recently completed a satiric novel called *Yeshiva Girls*, about rebellious teens at an Orthodox school in late 1970s New York City. Her memoir, *The Maternity Labyrinth*, was published by *Plain View Press* in 2010. She currently writes book reviews for *New York Journal of Books*.

Lori Barrett is a writer living in Chicago. Her work has appeared in *Salon, Bustle, Necessary Fiction, Barrelhouse, Paper Darts,* and *Entropy*. She has participated in Chicago's Live Lit events *That's All She Wrote* and *Tuesday Funk*. She volunteers as an assistant fiction editor at *Pithead Chapel*, and as a writing tutor at a local public high school.

Alexandra Nicole Benson is your basic type A, 20-something, who loves nothing more than listening to JT and Billie Eilish while studying for her never-ending nursing exams and working as a part-time nanny.

Wendy BooydeGraaff has been published in *Emrys Journal Online* (a list!), *The Emerson Review*, *Kveller*, *Third Wednesday*, *Rune Bear*, *Leopardskin & Limes*, and *SmokeLong Quarterly*, and is forthcoming in *Bending Genres*, *Jellyfish Review*, *So It Goes*, and *NOON*.

Kate R. Canter is a comic living in Los Angeles. See her perform at Tao Comedy Studio or check out her poorly updated website: Katercanter.com

Giugi Carminati is an intersectional feminist and woman's advocate. As an attorney, blogger, public speaker and hobbyist author, she spends her time explaining the patriarchy to all who will listen (and many who won't). She runs her law firm, The Woman's Lawyer, out of Denver, CO, and her blog *Argue Like a Girl* from wherever she has internet access. She speaks French, English, Italian, Spanish, and Cussing.

Belinda Carroll is a stand-up comedian, writer and vocalist living in Portland, Oregon. She's written for *Cracked.com*, *PQ Monthly* and *Huffington Post*, and founded the popular Portland Queer Comedy Festival. She is pro-mask, pro-BLM and anti-covidiot.

Joanna Collins is a Nashville poet and feminist who moonlights as a government attorney. Joanna took to the stage in "My Angry Vagina" and "Beat the Girl" in The Nashville Vagina Warriors' 2020 production of *The Vagina Monologues*. One day she will finish her Supreme Court musical.

Jamie Colson is a University of Washington graduate based in the Pacific Northwest. She is currently in the Cannabis Industry, and pursuing comedy. She loves gardening, and has a Permaculture Design Certification. Jamie is active in the community and loves her local comedy scene in Eugene, Oregon. Find her on Instagram @Jamie_the_budtender and on Twitter @jcolson_comedy.

Ellie Connor is a comedian from London, who enjoys writing articles for feminist comedy magazines such as *Succubus*, *Funny Women*, and *The Syndrome Mag*. Her main goal in life is to write a relatable hit song about eating pesto from the jar, but she needs to learn the jazz flute first.

Mia DeSantis is a Chicago comedian and comedy writer. In her spare time she loves petting dogs and eating a donut.

Daphne Dot works for a B2B publishing agency, and is sick to the teeth of "experts" giving advice about all the ways to deal with the crisis in a PG, professional manner.

Chika Ekemezie is a freelance writer, editor, and self-described "shit talker on the Internet," who writes about sex, politics, and everything in between. As a digital native, if it's on the Internet, she has something to say about it. She also co-runs a weekly newsletter called twenty-something, where she explores all the questions twenty-somethings are asking.

Jasmine Eftekhari writes because not everyone has the fortune to live in hell, or as everyone else calls it, "the Middle East."

Fernanda Estrada Argumedo is a Mexican journalist and podcast producer. Mostly, she is a feminist and a Christmas lover, but she has also worked for *Sonoro Media*, *Animal Político*, *Milenio Diario* and *W Radio*. Her work includes projects like gender studies' podcast *Rolas sin Roles* for conceptoradial.com and LGBT+ storytelling for *Queer Core*. Her very professional side project is watching every new season of *Grey's Anatomy*, which is a modern accomplishment, depending on who you ask.

Kristen Ferreira is a preschool teacher who dabbles in comedy and writing. When she isn't busy writing, dabbling in the comedy, and teaching, you will most likely find her watching murder mysteries or driving into parked cars.

Naomi Fitter escaped from Ohio at the age of 22. Her soothing midwestern voice has been described as "sexy," "librarian-like," and "nearly inaudible." When she's not telling jokes, she spends her time studying robots as a professor at Oregon State University.

Patricia Florio is the author of *My Two Mothers*, published by Phyllis Scott Publishing and numerous other essays, short stories and poems.

She is the founding publisher of *San Fedele Press*, a once-a-year literary anthology. She received her MFA from Wilkes University and taught as an English adjunct after she retired from her full-time job.

Linda Freund is a multimedia producer based in Spain, most recently on staff with *The Wall Street Journal*. She enjoys tap dancing and photographing Barcelona's modernist architecture (for best results: attempt at the same time).

Adina Gillett realized that her Poli-Sci degree from UCLA meant that she had no job skills, so she fell into a Technical Writer career thanks to a broken road of sketchy temp jobs. She spent most of two decades as a company member of Jet City Improv as a performer, teacher, corporate workshop trainer, and director of full-length improvised plays. Somewhere in the middle of that, Adina accidentally became a Hypnotherapist, and currently owns her own practice.

Katie Glauber Bush is a memoir and humor writer in Louisville, Kentucky. Katie's story "Sole Man" appears in the 2016 anthology *The Kindness of Strangers*. Her story "Queen of the May" appears in the 2015 anthology *Siblings: Our First Macrocosm*. Bush's story "Women's Work" appears in the anthology *Times They Were A-Changing*, a 2014 Finalist Indie Excellence Awards and a 2013 Finalist Foreword Reviews Book of the Year Award. Her work was honored by the San Francisco chapter of the National League of American Pen Women in 2012 and 2013.

Melody Dodd is an improv and stand-up comedian. She's lived in Japan and Italy but has called Eugene Oregon home since 1976. Watch for her in future performances with Out of Our Minds Improv.

Taylor Griggs is an Oregon-based writer working on both funny and serious stuff. She will probably eventually go to grad school. Follow her on Twitter at @taylorjgriggs.

Daien Guo is a writer living in Washington D.C. She has previously published her writing in *Furious Gravity*, *Little Patuxent Review*, *3Elements Literary Review*, *Columbia Journal of Asian Law*, and *Merlyn's Pen*. **Stacey Gustafson** is the bestselling author of *Are You Still Kidding Me?*

She's also a storyteller, blogger and stand-up comedian. Her short stories have appeared in *Chicken Soup for the Soul* and other online and print publications. She performs stand-up throughout the East Bay and lives in Pleasanton, CA with her college sweetheart, Mike, and a white furball named Stanley who loves peanut butter treats.

Laura Wheatman Hill lives in Portland, Oregon with her dentist and two children. She blogs about parenting, writes about everything, and teaches English and drama when not living in an apocalyptic dystopia. Her work has appeared on the Submittable blog, *Sammiches* and *Psych Meds, The Syndrome, Scary Mommy, Filter Free Parenting, Motherwell,* and *Distressed Millennial.*

Anndee Hochman is a journalist, essayist, storyteller and teaching artist in Philadelphia. She's the author of *Anatomies: A Novella and Stories,* and an essay collection, *Everyday Acts & Small Subversions: Women Reinventing Family, Community and Home.*

Bethany Grace Howe is a transgender woman, who upon completing her transition as a doctoral student now finds herself up to her ears in debt, misogyny, and people who think she's pushy for daring to use the prefix "Dr." before her name. In her free time, she's intentionally raising her daughter to be a social justice warrior who thinks calling her daddy "she" is perfectly normal, even when in a public restroom in Mississippi.

Laura Iodice resides with her husband in Syracuse, N.Y. Her work is featured in *The Furious Gazelle, Conclave Magazine, Litro U.S.* and *Litro U.K., Metafore Magazine, Crack the Spine Journal, Vending Machine, The Write Launch* and *Indolent Beast.* Most recently, she published her first children's book, *Where the Heart Lives.*

Leigh Anne Jasheway has been a comedy writer, stand-up comic, and humorous motivational speaker for 25 years (yes, she started in-utero!). She has 25 published books and regularly writes top 10 lists in the fog on strangers' bathroom mirrors. She won the Erma Bombeck Humor Writing Award for her true story on how her first mammogram caught on fire.

Gracie Kairis is a writer and semi-functioning adult living in the Pacific

Northwest. Her humor can be found on *Points in Case*, *Little Old Lady Comedy*, *Slackjaw*, and more. Follow her on Twitter @beaverkairis.

Lauren Klein is a writer and artist living in Toronto. She loves fallen leaves, full moons, and hanging out with the creatures she encounters in her neighborhood.

Laura Magnani. Born 1989, star sign: Syndrome. Distinguishing features: never shuts up (she tries but must always say what's on her mind. She loves red wine and beers sitting on church steps. She never leaves the house without red lipstick or cynicism.

Eloise O'Loane has equal love for going to barre and going to the bar. She's passionate for peanut butter, writing, and memes respectively. Not to mention, kinda funny.

Meg Riley is a copywriter for *Murray's Cheese*, and when not writing blogs about Brie, wine pairings, and olive oil, she pens personal essays about her sex life. She has a B.A. in English from Fordham University, a background in publishing, and a lot of irrelevant knowledge about cheese.

Jennifer Scully is a lawyer in Seattle, Washington who enjoys cooking, looking out the window, annoying her teenagers, and using up all the WiFi.

Kathryn Sadakierski's writing has appeared in *ActiveMuse*, *The Bangor Literary Journal*, *The Ekphrastic Review*, *Nine Muses Poetry*, *Teachers of Vision*, *Dime Show Review*, *The Decadent Review*, *Visual Verse*, and *iō Literary Journal*. She has a B.A. from Bay Path University, and is currently pursuing her Master's degree.

Sara Savusa is a Chicago based performer and director. She moved to Chicago from Hawai`i, and is thankful her family continues to mail island snacks.

Sarah Shamim is a high-school student, activist, writer, poet, performer, and *Stranger Things* enthusiast. She runs her own mental health movement called *The Ranjish Project*. One of her biggest aims is to make climate fiction and journalism common in South Asia. Apart from the climate, her work focuses on culture, gender, and politics.

Brooke Stanicki is a new writer with published fiction and poetry. She has been featured in Indolent Book's *What Rough Beast* poetry series and has upcoming fiction in the anthology *Tymes Goe By Turnes* by *Arcane Publishing*. When not writing, she is a pre-medical student studying at Johns Hopkins University in Baltimore, MD.

Marie Steinwachs has been writing essays for years but you wouldn't know unless you were interested in waste. She has broadened her topic range since retiring last year from an environmental career. She lives and laughs in North Central Florida.

Christina Tang-Bernas has been published in *Soft Cartel*, *DNA Magazine*, and *Brevity Magazine*. When she isn't writing, she engages a different part of her literary brain by copyediting academic manuscripts.

Regina Velázquez is a displaced Southerner living in New England. Editorial production manager by day and writer by night, she spends her precious leisure time finding new ways to embarrass her two kids.

Courtney Watson is a writer and college professor in Roanoke, Virginia. Her work has been published in *100 Word Story*, *Bookends Review*, *Long Story*, *Short*, and more.

Linda White lives in Alberta, Canada, where she spends time gardening, camping, reading and writing She gets her ideas for essays while walking her dogs.

Katherine Wilson is an actress and writer living in Italy. She goes on Italian TV regularly to "explain" US politics and culture from an American prospective, a job that requires multiple espressos, proseccos, and talented makeup artists. Her memoir, *Only in Naples*, tells about her experiences as an American feminist in the kitchen of her Neapolitan mother-in-law.

Christie Withanie is a writer and entertainer with a focus on equity and NSFW humor.

Carmen Woodruff is a professional writer, singer and all-around let's live a good life enthusiast. Immersed in the comedy scene as a publicist for many years, Carmen recently made steps of her own onto the funny stage as a budding improvisational performer. She spends her days and nights as a communications consultant, a contemporary vocal coach and a college professor, stretching her widest to inspire tomorrow's generation to go in the direction of their dreams with a droplet of humor and lots of pizzazz.

Hayley Zablotsky is a writer based in Northern California. Her work has recently been published in *Narratively* and *The Belladonna Comedy*. She's working on her debut novel, a screenplay, and a recipe for the perfect grilled cheese sandwich.

Halle Zander has taught performance poetry through the High School High Scholar program and competed at the 5C Poetry SLAM team in college. She spends too much of her paychecks on lattes and uses Cruise Control when going 25 mph. Her biggest passion in life is crafting stories in compelling ways that enlighten and expand peoples' perspectives in the world.

ACKNOWLEDGEMENTS

It's 2020. In a year that has been trying for so many reasons we've struggled, we've adapted, we've grown, and we also decided to show you our wits.

None of this would have been possible without the amazing help of many people.

For collecting the stories, communicating with the authors and editing the material, while always respecting the writers' voice and their unique experience, thank you Leigh Anne Jasheway and Chika Ekemezie. We so appreciate your work.

For their editorial support, thanks are due to: Katherine Shaw, Janet Livingstone and Carmen Woodruff. Your thorough reading, discussions and suggestions were valuable to the realization of this project.

For the constant oversight of digital content, project management and incredible patience: Thank you, Tiffany Burton.

To our board members - Linda Benson, Raelene Bushbeck, O'Dealya Price, Sophia Woolery and Janet Livingstone - who have supervised, discussed and supported the project, a huge thank you.

Finally, a special acknowledgement to our writers and readers, to whom this book is dedicated: May laughter remind us that, as long as we find humor in life, we are powerful beyond measure.

The Directress, Silvia Bajardi

ABOUT US:
THE SYNDROME MAG

The Syndrome Mag is an online magazine featuring real stories shared by women.

Through personal accounts and social media, we provide comic relief complete with funny memes and commentary based on the ever-entertaining current events of today.

The Syndrome project from its early days has grown rapidly and is on its way to become a global phenomenon rooted in the female perspective.

We represent an inclusive community of intergenerational women spanning the gamut of cultural, geographical, socioeconomic, religious, and professional backgrounds, as well as sexual orientation and identity.

The Syndrome Mag provides workshops and live corporate comedy shows that highlight difficult topics relating to gender inequality in the workplace.

Please follow us on:

@thesyndromemag

https://thesyndromemag.com

DONATE

Invest in gender equality work today!

Help us to continue our work and empower all women through laughter and comedy.

Go to: https://thesyndromemag.com/donate/

The Syndrome Mag is a not-for-profit 501(c)(3) organization, tax ID 82-3198998. All donations to us are tax-deductible.

CREDITS

This book is supported, in part, by a grant from the Washington State Arts Commission and the National Endowment for the Arts.

WASHINGTON STATE
ARTS COMMISSION

Made in the USA
Monee, IL
08 January 2021

56899823R00125